Angels
Among Us

*Powerful Friends
Who Guard, Guide, and Protect*

Angels
Among Us

*Powerful Friends
Who Guard, Guide, and Protect*

Zoe M. Hicks

Copyright © 2024 by Encouragement Unlimited, Inc.

Atlanta, GA

Printed in the United States of America

All Rights Reserved

Cover Design by Virginia Sowell

Scripture quotations are from New Revised Standard Version Bible, copyright © 1989 National Council of the Churches of Christ in the United States of America. Used by permission. All rights reserved worldwide.

Paperback ISBN 979-8-218-47945-9

For the Angels—Human & Divine

Make friends with the angels, who though invisible are always with you. Often invoke them, constantly praise them, and make good use of their help and assistance in all your temporal affairs.

St. Francis de Sales

Table of Contents

Foreword and Acknowledgments 1
1 Are Angels Real? 5
2 Angel Allies 15
3 Angels of Encouragement, Comfort, and Prophecy 29
4 Angels with Healing in Their Wings 39
5 Heaven's Ushers 51
6 Angels and Travelers 59
7 Angels and Children 71
8 Assignments and Hierarchies 79
9 Angels Singing and Worshiping 87
10 The Comforting Angels 95
11 Heaven's Warriors 105
12 The Devil's Angels 117
13 The Angels We Know and Love 127
Prayer 139
Endnotes 141

Foreword and Acknowledgments

Why write a book about angels? Most of us would acknowledge their existence, but when it comes to paying any attention to them, we don't. We don't see that they matter to us. Perhaps we consider them important in Biblical times, but not anymore. Perhaps we think they are too involved with other activities to be interested in us. Perhaps we think they only aid and assist missionaries and ministers.

I will admit to being in the category of those who rarely thought about them until a good friend whose credibility was unquestioned had a personal encounter with angels. As he was telling me about his experience, I was mesmerized. I wanted to know more and went to the theology library at Emory University to see what I could find. I was hoping to find information about people's personal encounters with angels, but all I found were theological treatises and tomes reviewing angel stories in the Bible. I asked the reference librarian if he could find a bibliography on angels for me.

From the bibliography, I began to find recent books written by people who had encountered angels or interviewed those who had. As I began to share some of my stories with friends, I learned several of my friends had their own angel experiences. Although some of the stories were more in the near-death experience category and therefore not includable in this book, others were exciting adventures these people had with our heavenly friends. I am honored to have their permission to share their stories with you here.

I think we do ourselves and those we love a disservice by ignoring the angels that God has sent to help us in so many ways. Hebrews 1:14 says, "Are not all angels spirits in the divine service, sent to serve for the sake of those who are to inherit salvation?"

In researching this book, I have come to appreciate angels in ways I never have before. I know they have saved my life. You will read my story in the chapter on angels and travelers.

We can ask God to send them to protect us or our loved ones from getting in harm's way. We can ask him to send them to influence those we love in positive ways.

We can pray for them to be divine interpreters between us and those with whom we are negotiating, instructing, or counseling. One grandmother even prayed for God to send angels to entertain her three-year-old grandson to take his mind off of his ear infection. Soon after that, the grandson came running in to tell his grandmother that five angels dressed in green had been dancing in front of him. No one in the family had ever mentioned angels to this little fellow. He was adamant in defending his story of the dancing angels any time anyone brought it up. It seems the ministry of angels is inexhaustible.

I hope this book will encourage you to call for angelic help any time you need protection, guidance, or assistance. The holy angels are our friends, and like human friends, we must nourish and cherish the relationship to get the most out of it. As you read, I pray for an angel to open your eyes to the whole realm of supernatural help that is there for the asking.

As with all books, this book could never have happened without the help of many others. From the reference librarian at the Emory School of Theology to those precious friends who shared their stories with me, to the authors of all the books I read about angels, to all others who edited, typed, formatted, printed, and designed the cover of this book, I say thank you: although thank you is not enough. You are all the best. Special thanks to Virginia Sowell for designing the cover, Carrie Kroll for making helpful suggestions about the content, Tamara Cribley for formatting, and Chris Knight for editing.

And thank you to my precious husband, Charles (aka "Smoky"), who gave me the time and encouragement to keep going on this project until it was completed. Most of all, thank you to our amazing, incredible God, who created the angels and sends them to help us and get us out of all kinds of difficult situations.

Zoe M. Hicks

Are Angels Real?

"Angels are all around us, all of the time, in the very air we breathe."

Eileen Elias Freeman

When I recently shared with a friend that I was writing a book about angels, she asked, "Is it fiction?" Was she putting angels in the same category as fairies, elves, trolls, leprechauns, and flying reindeer? Some do. To add to the confusion, popular entertainment such as Walt Disney's *Angels in the Outfield* makes them look fictional.

In Disney's movie, the Los Angeles baseball team, the LA Angels were in last place in their division halfway through the season. A ten-year-old foster child named Roger, an avid Angels fan, asked God to please send help so the Angels could win some games. As Roger and his buddy, J.P., watched another dismal performance by their team, an angel named Al zoomed in to tell them God had heard Roger's prayer.

Everything suddenly began to look dramatically different on the field. With the next pitch, as the opposing batter swung and made solid contact with the ball, sending it high enough to be a home run, two mighty angels (invisible to everyone except Roger) swooshed in to pick up the Angels' center fielder and lift him high enough to catch the ball before it sailed out of the park.

The Angels' announcer was stunned. "Did you see that?" he yelled. "That will be seen on every sports channel for decades! How in the world did he do that?" The center fielder later said it was like an unseen power had lifted him higher than he could have ever jumped to catch the ball.

Then, in the bottom of the ninth inning, as the Angels trailed by one run, the worst batter on the team stepped up to the plate. The Angels had one man on base. The only way they were going to win the game was for this guy to hit a home run. The pitcher hurled the ball. It rocketed toward home plate. The batter positioned his bat, and suddenly, a mighty angel (complete with wings, a halo, and a white robe) appeared and put his arms around the batter, helping him make the swing of a lifetime. The ball almost disintegrated as it made its way completely out of the ballpark, sealing the deal for the Angels.

In one game after another, the LA Angels defeated every team they encountered with superhuman athleticism provided by the angelic help Roger prayed in. The angels always appeared at just the right moment and usually assisted the weakest players on the team, who, with their help, looked like superstars. The angels also managed to trick the opposing team into committing ridiculous errors, making them look more like stooges than professional athletes.

This feel-good movie has a very happy ending, with the Angels winning the pennant. Roger and J.P., foster kids, also get their happy ending when the Angels' manager adopts them. However, the movie leaves viewers with the impression that angels are like Superman or Captain America, fictional characters stepping in to rescue the underdog whenever they're summoned.

No wonder so many people think angels are just imaginary superheroes. Yet, the Bible, the inspired Word of God, tells us angels are real. In fact, the Old Testament mentions angels 108 times, and the New Testament mentions them 165 times. Angels delivered important messages to Abraham, Daniel, Zacharias (father of John the Baptist), and Mary, the mother of Jesus. They appear in glorious celebration to sing in the birth of God's son. They fought battles (one angel knocked out 185,000 enemy troops in a single night during the reign of King Hezekiah of Judah). They strengthened the Lord Jesus after his temptation by the devil in the wilderness. They guarded Jesus's tomb after his crucifixion. Angels sang glory and honor to the King of Kings and Lord of Lords in Revelation, "And all the angels stood around the throne...singing, 'Amen! Blessing and glory and wisdom and thanksgiving and honor and power and might be to our God for ever and ever! Amen.'"[1] Jesus himself told his disciples he could call down ten thousand angels to deliver him from the pain and agony of the crucifixion if he chose to do so.

The Bible tells us that angels are real, powerful, and intelligent beings who God sends to minister to those who are to inherit salvation.[2] So, for those of us who believe the Bible is the inspired Word of God, we have no choice but to believe in angels.

What Are Angels, Anyway?

Let's take a moment and consider what angels are. Most of us get our ideas about angels from artists who've drawn them through the centuries. They have wings, halos, flowing white robes, and maybe even a sword, shield, or spear. Sometimes, the artists draw angels as chubby cherubs holding harps. These forms, which angels can take should they need to, are like costumes to us. Yes, perhaps we don a costume for a party or special event, but we are not the person we're pretending to be, and once the party is over, we ditch the outfit and return to normal.

Angels are spiritual beings with no bodies of their own. They can assume any form needed. They are minds without bodies; we will consider what this means later. One writer envisioned a giant wardrobe room in heaven outfitting angels sent on earthly missions. For example, an angel being sent on a mission to a rancher in Wyoming and needing to look like a local might request boots, a ten-gallon hat, blue jeans, and a plaid shirt and would need a beat-up pickup truck to arrive on the scene. An angel needing to appear as a doctor to someone in the hospital might request a white jacket, stethoscope, chart, and a pen.

Many of the testimonies we will hear involve someone who initially thought he or she was dealing with an ordinary human being who fit into the scene. Later, because the person who helped simply disappeared after rendering the necessary assistance, the recipient knew it had to be an angel. Or, perhaps an unseen force moved someone out of harm's way in the nick of time or took over controls in a car or plane, much to the surprise of the driver or pilot. Those telling the stories knew these experiences involved supernatural deliverances.

Defending the Reality of Angels

How would we present a case for the reality of angels to those who don't believe in God? As we will see, angels usually work behind the scenes, *incognito*. While they occasionally assume bodies and appear to those who need to see them, very few have had the pleasure. Many more, however, have had an experience that saved their lives, the life of a child, or put them in direct contact with someone who changed the course of their lives with no rational explanation for the experience. How, then, can we explain what happened to these individuals?

Fourteenth-century philosopher William of Ockham said if we cannot explain observed phenomena in any other way, then something unperceived must have caused it. This reasoning has been followed by careful, cautious scientists and philosophers ever since.[3]

Nuclear physicists use this argument concerning imperceptible elementary particles. In many of the following stories, those who have shared their experiences cannot attribute their deliverance or encounter to anything known or perceived.

Another argument for the non-believer is the "great chain of being." This can be regarded as either a philosophical doctrine concerning the arrangement of nature or a theological doctrine explaining God's design of a perfect and orderly universe. The argument goes that because the universe proceeds from things lifeless (rocks and minerals) to things living with no brains (plants) to things living with brains but no powers of judgment and reasoning (animals) to things living with brains that have powers of reasoning and judgment and spirits (humans), there must be something above humans before God to fill the gap or complete the picture of the orderly arrangement of nature. Angels, spirit beings unconstrained by bodies, would do that, completing the gap in the great chain of being. Minds or spirits unconstrained by bodies can do things minds constrained by bodies cannot do. A mind constrained by a body can only be in one place at a time. A mind unconstrained by a body can be in more than one place at a time, much like a corporation formed in Delaware can also be doing business in Texas.

Arguing Against Angels

Who would argue against the possibility of angels? Materialists believe nothing exists except corporeal bodies, substances occupying physical space by their bulk or extension. Angels are incorporeal beings. Therefore, say the materialists, they don't exist.

Aristotle and Thomas Aquinas, both immaterialists, disagreed. They believed that the failure to acknowledge the possibility of spiritual beings stemmed from not distinguishing the actions of the human brain between sense perception and imagination on the one hand and intellection and understanding on the other. According to this view, intellection—understanding and thinking—is not the act of the brain. It is the act of an incorporeal power humans possess.[4]

Angels—beings without bodies—can also possess intellection since a physical body isn't required.

In his book *Encounters with Angels*, L.W. Northrup gives several reasons why people have stopped believing in angels or at least decided they're no longer worth knowing about.

First, when Soviet cosmonauts returned from orbiting Earth, they announced they had not found evidence of God.

This corroborates their atheistic philosophy. Later, in 1985, when Soviet cosmonauts said they had witnessed a band of glowing angels—seven giant figures with wings and mist-like halos—they later changed their testimony and said when all of the facts were in, they did not see angels but creatures descended from a race of humanoids who shed their bodies when they reached the top of the evolutionary ladder.

Second, humanistic philosophy has been so universally believed that many people can only conceive of one world (not both earth and heaven). They live completely in the domain of the existing corporeal world and believe that death ends our existence. God does not exist to them, nor do his ministers, the angels.

Third, people have substituted extraterrestrial creatures for the angels. Despite all the advances in science and technology, humans cannot seem to shake the belief in beings of superhuman nature. Many people seem to believe that other planets are inhabited and that any day now, they'll appear to us in some kind of invasion from outer space. Films like *E.T. the Extra-Terrestrial* and *Close Encounters of the Third Kind* were extremely popular. In addition, people want to believe in UFOs and want to think that these extraterrestrial creatures are benevolent and intelligent.

Fourth, angels have been degraded as childish notions and comic misrepresentations, depicted as chubby little creatures flying off Christmas trees. Karl Barth, the great modern theologian, stated that he detested paintings depicting the infant Jesus with a veritable kindergarten of prancing babies amusing themselves in different ways, yet all contriving in some way to also look pious.

Fifth, to many, the loss of angels is irrelevant. So what if there are angels, they say? What does that mean for me? Religious thinking is completely out of their sphere of existence. They have never given it any thought and don't plan to. Eternal things have no place in their philosophy of life.

Finally, we live in such an affluent society that we have no need for angels. If we were to face the mouths of lions or the fires of martyrdom, we might be more interested in them.[5]

The Minds of Angels

Angels get their intellect from God. Aristotle believed angels were ranked according to the number of ideas God gave each one. An angel of a higher order would have more ideas about greater subjects (the universe as compared to ideas about humankind, for example) than an angel of a lower order. Angels in a higher order know all of what the angels lower than themselves know and some of what angels of a higher order know.

The ideas or information each possesses, given by God, is infallible. Angels' knowledge is instantaneous and certain, but unlike God, they are not omniscient. For example, angels do not know what goes on in the hearts and minds of individuals, nor do they know what will happen to the physical cosmos.

Their knowledge includes the physical cosmos. The limited human intellect can know the cosmos through sense perception, reflection, and reasoning, but angels know such things because of the ideas God implanted in their created natures.[6] Human knowledge is imperfect; angelic knowledge is not.

Summary

As we can see, good reasons apart from the Bible exist for believing in angels. Hundreds of thousands of testimonies (some of which you will read here) involve deliverance from every imaginable danger with no rational explanation for how it happened. This points to supernatural assistance. We call it the ministry of angels.

2

Angel Allies

"Are not all angels spirits in the divine service, sent to serve for the sake of those who are to inherit salvation?"

Hebrews 1:14

This past summer, I was in London, England. While there, my family and I toured the Churchill war rooms, where Winston Churchill directed Britain's war effort during World War II, strategizing with military and diplomatic leaders from his protected bunker.

Adjacent to the war rooms is a museum with memorabilia, posters, strategic dates, and initiatives for us to enjoy. One of the posters featured Britain's allies during World War II, noting that Churchill knew he could not win the war without help from his allies, the Soviet Union and the United States. In fact, when the United States entered the war in December 1941, Churchill reportedly said, "So, we have won the war after all."

The Importance of Allies

What do military allies do for each other?

1. They provide military assistance during wartime. This includes providing troops, equipment, and strategic coordination. During World War II, the Allied Powers (including the United States, Britain, and the Soviet Union) collaborated by sharing intelligence, military offenses, troops, and supplies.

2. They provide economic aid and supplies. Before entering WWII, the United States sent financial aid to the Soviet Union, providing crucial resources to help them fight against Nazi Germany. Sometimes, allies simply offer economic assistance and supplies to help support a war effort, such as the United States is currently doing in the war between Ukraine and Russia.

3. Allies often work to build international support for their cause and negotiate favorable outcomes. In 1990–1991, a coalition of nations led by the United States worked together to secure United Nations resolutions and international support for the liberation of Kuwait from Iraqi occupation.

4. Allies share intelligence and information to enhance their military and strategic capabilities. When they discover, through code-breaking or other endeavors, strategies, or enemy plans, they can share the information to assist in ultimate victory.

5. Allies often provide logistical support for each other, such as access to bases, transportation, and infrastructure to facilitate the movement of troops and supplies. During World War II, Liberia provided key logistic support to the United States by allowing US planes to land on their airstrips, where they could refuel and rest before heading to Europe with the necessary supplies and troops.

Allies are critical in times of war and even in times of peace. One of the most famous books on war, *The Art of War* by Sun Tzu, emphasizes the importance of unity and cooperation among allies. Sun Tzu argues that when allies work seamlessly together, they become a formidable force that is difficult to defeat. Sun Tzu also stresses the need for constant communication and coordination with allies and warns against neglecting or taking them for granted.

Spiritual Allies

In the spiritual realm, although we have adversaries, we also have powerful angelic allies assisting and protecting us even though we cannot see them. Angels can protect us from enemy attacks, whether they are armies of a foreign government, smaller gangs, or individuals targeting us for whatever reason. They also protect us from spiritual attacks, which may be their most important level of protection.

In 2 Kings, chapter 6, we learn that the king of Aram was at war with Israel. The prophet Elisha, gaining intelligence from the throne of heaven, would pass on the plans of the king of Aram to the king of Israel. The king of Israel alerted the points of the intended attack, thwarting the enemy's plans.

The king of Aram was greatly disturbed and believed there must be spies in his leadership team leaking information to the enemy. When he questioned his military leaders, one of his officers responded, "My lord king, it is Elisha, the prophet in Israel, who tells the king of Israel the words that you speak in your bedchamber."

The Aramean military leaders were ordered to find and seize Elisha. They learned he was in Dothan and sent a great army with horses and chariots to surround the city at night and bring back the troubling prophet.

The next morning, Elisha's servant woke early and went out, terrified to see that a great military force surrounded the city. Running inside to find his master, he cried, "Alas, my master! What shall we do?"

Elisha was not disturbed. He knew he had angelic allies greater and more powerful than the military forces that had come for him. He first assured his servant, "Don't be afraid, for there are more with us than there are with them."

He then prayed, "Oh Lord, please open his eyes that he may see." When the Lord opened the spiritual eyes of the servant, he could see that the mountain was full of horses and chariots of fire, armed men with shields and flashing spears, all around Elisha.

As the Arameans came down from the mountain to attack, Elisha prayed, "Strike this people, please, with blindness." The Lord answered, and Elisha approached the blind leader and said, "This is not the way, and this is not the city; follow me, and I will bring you to the man whom you seek."

Elisha led them to Samaria, where Israel's king resided. Elisha then prayed, "Lord, open the eyes of these men so that they may see." As the Arameans opened their eyes, they saw they were inside enemy territory. On Elisha's counsel, the king of Israel did not kill them but prepared a great feast for them and, after they had eaten their fill, sent them back to their king. The king of Aram, receiving his army back intact and with a tale to tell, never again raided the land of Israel.[7]

Two observations from this incredible story:

1. Elisha told his servant that there were more allies than adversaries. At first, the servant could only see the enemy army, but once God opened his eyes, he could see the Lord's host of heavenly angel warriors all around, protecting his master and himself. We know from God's Word that one-third of the heavenly hosts rebelled with Satan against God.[8] That means two-thirds of the heavenly host remained faithful to the God they loved. So, yes, there are always more allies than adversaries.

2. Elisha's servant did not see the allies until God enabled him to see them at the request of Elisha. Rarely do we see the angel allies with our physical eyes, but we can get into the habit of seeing them with our spiritual eyes and thanking God they are there. The prophet Nahum gives us a vivid description of the angel armies: "The shields of his warriors are red; his soldiers are clothed in crimson. The metal on the chariots flashes on the day when he musters them; the chargers prance."[9]

When we are in harm's way and ask God to command his angels concerning us, he sends fierce warriors, not chubby cherubs with harps. Sometimes, only those who are attacking see the mighty warriors and are frightened enough to retreat, not wanting to engage with such intimidating warrior angels.

How Our Unseen Allies Work

There are so many testimonials of miraculous protection and deliverance from our men and women in the military that we can be assured angel allies are at work. After all, it is in times of warfare that we are closest to our military allies. When peace reigns, we know they are there, but they aren't actively engaged in our physical protection.

The first question is: do we have to call on the angels to help us? We certainly call on our allies to help us in wartime. Although it appears there are times when God just sends the angels without any human asking for them, most of the testimonies I have read involve either the person, a friend, or a family member calling for help, claiming God's promise of protection in Psalm 91[10] or elsewhere in his Word.

Iraqi Soldier Ready to Launch His Grenade, Flees

Chaplain Carey H. Cash, United States Navy, is a battalion chaplain to infantry Marines. In his book, *A Table in the Presence*, he shares miraculous stories of deliverance from the men with whom he was privileged to serve. With tears in their eyes, they told him God sent angels to protect them in their time of greatest need.

One such story relayed by Corporal Zebulon Batke, a grenade launcher told of an encounter with the enemy where it got so bad he could feel the bullets whizzing past him. He could see men running all around—on rooftops, walls, everywhere. He thought he would be hit, but something just kept him going.

Something told Corporal Batke to look to his right, and when he did, he saw an Iraqi soldier not more than twenty-five feet away, ready to launch his rocket-propelled grenade right at Corporal Batke. What happened next, reported Batke, was simply unexplainable. Before Batke could get his weapon turned around and aimed at the soldier, the soldier jumped up as if he had seen a ghost. He looked at a fellow Iraqi soldier nearby, shouting and waving frantically. The two men took off, running as fast as they could into a darkened alley.

The soldiers never looked back. Instead of taking a point-blank shot into the idling American Humvee manned by Corporal Batke, the Iraqis ran for their lives. What had they seen? Why did they not shoot their missile? Why did they run for their lives?

One of the men with Batke, Corporal Ayani Dawson, who became a Christian just weeks earlier, grinned as he explained things to Chaplain Cash. "Chaplain, remember those angels, the ones your wife talked about—the legions? They surrounded us. I should be dead, Chaplain, but God was with me."[11]

Sergeant Assists Medics on the Front Lines

Sergeant George H. Barclay served in World War II in General Patton's 320th Infantry, US Army. His family constantly feared he would not return home, especially when his entire outfit was cut off from the rest of the army during the Battle of the Bulge. The media reported that half of his company had been killed.

Finally, however, his wife received a letter from him saying that God had given him Psalm 91, and he now had absolute certainty that he would come home without any injuries. He was so certain of his divine protection that when the medics asked for volunteers to go to the front lines and bring back the wounded, he volunteered and made repeated trips under extreme enemy fire to rescue those who would have otherwise died.

Although he received the Bronze Star Award for bravery, he insisted it wasn't his courage but God's covenant promise of angelic protection in Psalm 91 that enabled him to do what he did. When he came home without a scratch, it was obvious the angels bore him up on their hands, allowing no evil to befall him.[12]

Angelic Allies in Times of Peace

What can we expect from our angel allies in times of peace? Are they still active and working on our behalf? Yes! We know from the Bible they guide and warn, bringing wise counsel and encouragement and protection from spiritual attacks designed to bring us down. Even though we might not be militarily at war with our adversaries, there is always a spiritual war going on for our welfare, souls, and those we love. We need our angel allies as we fight on our knees.

Angels Guiding

When God tapped Moses to bring the children of Israel to the Promised Land, he promised to send his angel ahead of them to lead.[13] After herding the Israelites through the Red Sea and demolishing Pharaoh's army, God knew his people needed time to learn how to live as a free people. He kept them at Mount Sinai for over a year, giving them the Ten Commandments and the law, instructing them on temple worship, and teaching the priests how to bless and instruct the people. When it was time to set out from Mount Sinai to the Promised Land, God did not expect Moses to figure out which route he should take or how to get where they were going. Not only did God send his angel to go ahead of Moses and the children of Israel, but he promised to drive out all of the foreign forces standing in their way.

Do angels guide us today as well? While they don't appear as a cloud by day and a pillar of fire by night, they are working to help God's children get to their own promised lands. The CEO of a child welfare organization on whose board I sit told us she was praying about where a new program we were implementing should be initiated. During this time, she had several phone calls from one particular area of the state requesting our assistance. She said it was like God was saying, "We need you up here! Start here." I believe angels influenced those callers to guide the CEO.

Angels Warning

When Barak, king of Moab, was terrified of the Israelites camped on his doorstep en route to the Promised Land, he sent for the prophet, Balaam, to curse the Israelites so he could defeat them. He promised great riches if Balaam would curse his enemy.

Balaam, famed for his prophetic record of blessing and cursing, told Barak he could only curse what God told him. He took the king's request to the Lord, who told him not to go with Barak's men to curse the Israelites. Barak, undeterred by this response, sent more important men and promises of greater rewards to Balaam to request his presence for a curse.

Again, Balaam took the request to the Lord, who told him to go but to say only what the Lord told him to say. Although the Lord told Balaam to go, he was not pleased that Balaam had made a second request when God had already made his will known. Balaam was hoping God would change his mind so Balaam could claim the reward.

As Balaam journeyed to Barak's city, his donkey saw an angel with a drawn sword in the path and turned aside. Balaam struck the donkey and made her get back on the path. The donkey stepped aside two more times to avoid the angel with Balaam striking her each time. The third time, God caused the donkey to speak, and she asked Balaam why he struck her when she had been his faithful donkey for all of these years. God then revealed, through the angel, that Balaam's heart was not right. Balaam confessed his sin and offered to turn back.

God's angel told Balaam to continue but not to accept the riches Barak had promised.

He should say only what God told him to say.

Balaam wound up blessing the Israelites instead of cursing them, much to the dismay of Barak. Had the angel not revealed his lust to him, allowing him to acknowledge his sin, he might have taken the offered gold and lost his life.[14]

Do angels warn us today? Yes, most often through the strong thoughts they bring to us. We ignore these to our own detriment.

Angels Providing Aid and Logistical Support

Allies provide aid and logistical support. Do angels do that for us today? Yes, through the strong thoughts and urges they place in our minds. Angels are influencers. Even as angels can protect us through their warnings, they can also influence us to take positive actions that provide aid and logistical support for our allies on the front lines or for us if we're the ones on the front lines.

One of my favorite stories involves Helen Roseveare, a medical doctor missionary in equatorial Africa who had just delivered a premature baby. Unfortunately, the baby's mother, who also had another little girl, died in childbirth.

Later that day, the missionary had story time with the children of the village she was serving, and she shared with the children about the baby, her sister, and their mother. She told the children they had to have a hot water bottle to keep the infant alive. As the children began to pray after the story, one little girl, Ruth, prayed, "Dear God, we need a hot water bottle today to keep the baby alive, and please send a doll for her big sister while you are at it."

Helen didn't know what to do. She couldn't imagine anyone back home sending a hot water bottle to her in equatorial Africa. Later that day, however, a care package arrived from the United States. She called the children together to help her open the box and see what surprises awaited. The children clapped and squealed in glee as colorful hats, dresses, and toys emerged from the box. Even candies and dried fruits were included, to everyone's delight. As the missionary dug deeper, she felt something rubbery in her hand. What could it be? She grabbed it tightly and pulled it out of the box, gasping as it became apparent that it was a hot water bottle. Ruth, the little girl who prayed for it, said excitedly, "Keep looking, doctor. There has to be a doll in there, too."

Sure enough, the next thing pulled from the box was a beautiful doll, all dressed up and ready to give to the infant's big sister.

That box was packed months earlier. Who would think a hot water bottle would be needed in such a permanently hot climate? An angel surely put a strong thought into one of the women who helped to shop for items to pack in the box.[15]

Sometimes, we are on the receiving end of the aid, and sometimes we are on the sending end. Let's listen to our strong thoughts and urges because it could well be an angel ally wanting to provide valuable intel.

Summary

For the most part, we Christians have not been taught to work with our angel allies. We fail to ask God to send them to help us. And yet, allies are crucial to ensure a formidable force against the enemy as the famous general Sun Tzu reminds us. We should never ignore them or fail to ask for their help.

Even as military allies meant the difference in Britain being able to survive Hitler's onslaught in World War II, we simply cannot, without the help of our heavenly allies, be victorious in critical battles we face here on earth, whether those battles are physical threats or spiritual attacks. Our formidable enemy watches us to see where we are vulnerable and attacks us there. One pastor reported the spiritual battle going on in his mind, tempting him to be unfaithful to his wife. He called on God to send angel allies to come and help him. He said the battle was so intense that he even prayed for the archangel, Michael, to come to his aid. With his spiritual eyes, he saw the holy angels beating back demons. Soon, he reported, the angel allies had routed the enemy and delivered him from committing a great sin.[16] That was one wise pastor. May we all follow his good example; God doesn't intend for us to fight alone.

3

Angels of Encouragement, Comfort, and Prophecy

"Believers, look up – take courage. The angels are nearer than you think."

Billy Graham

Angels are sent by God to tell humans about future events that affect them or those for whom they have responsibility. The angel Gabriel was sent to tell Zacharias, a priest in ancient Israel, that he and his wife Elizabeth would have a son in their old age who would be named John. We know him as John the Baptist. Gabriel was then sent to a young virgin named Mary to tell her she would be the mother of the Son of God. Then, an angel appeared to Mary's fiancé, Joseph, to advise him not to break his engagement to Mary. After the baby was born, Joseph was again visited by an angel to warn him about a plot to kill all male babies under age two.

In the Old Testament, angels were sent to Abraham and Sarah to tell them they would be parents in their old age; an angel was sent to Hagar to tell her about the future of her son,

Ishmael, when she was close to despair; two angels warned Abraham's nephew, Lot, to flee the city of Sodom, where he lived, because God was about to destroy it. An angel was sent to the prophet Daniel to give him insights about future events. God still sends angels to share the future and to encourage us.

Outcomes of Court Case Prophesied:

David Green, founder and CEO of Hobby Lobby, tells a story in his book, *Business Not by the Book*, about a US Supreme Court case involving Hobby Lobby. In 2014, Hobby Lobby sued the Health and Human Services Department of the US Government, which required Hobby Lobby to provide and facilitate four life-terminating drugs and devices in their health insurance plan. In other words, Hobby Lobby would either have to pay for abortions for its employees or pay severe fines for noncompliance. Hobby Lobby argued their religious freedom protected them from complying with the federal mandate.

    David Green stated he did not know how the case would turn out, but he had surrendered Hobby Lobby to God. The wait, however, as the case worked its way up to the Supreme Court, was "excruciating."

    Hobby Lobby's general counsel, Peter Dobelbower, went to Washington, DC, to present oral arguments in the case. While in DC, Peter and his wife decided to take a Sunday taxi ride to a museum they wanted to see. At the end of the ride, their Nigerian driver turned around and handed them a receipt and a card that read, "Do you know Jesus?"

    Peter was surprised. He said, "Yes, thank you, we do. I'd like to ask you to pray for me. I am with Hobby—"

The driver cut him off mid-sentence and said, "Yes, I know who you are. This is your divine appointment, and you will win."

"What?" asked Peter.

"This is your divine appointment, and you will win."

Peter couldn't believe what he was hearing. He and his wife sat in the back seat of the car, crying. They realized God sent a special messenger to tell them how the case would turn out. Although he looked like a regular taxi driver, he had to be an angel sent by God to deliver the message of encouragement and prophecy to Hobby Lobby's chief legal officer.

Three months later, on June 30, 2014, the Supreme Court ruled five to four in favor of Hobby Lobby.[17]

An Angel Comforts and Encourages a Young Boy

Six-year-old Dale came home from school on Friday afternoon excited about the weekend. On Saturday, he would get to spend time with his dad, an engineer and a pilot in the Air Force Reserves. Dad and Dale had discussed his occasional weekend trips to practice flying, and his dad had told Dale that he would always come back in a "day or two."

Dale rushed into the kitchen to see his mom, showing her his schoolwork with silver stars. He knew his dad would be home soon, and they were going fishing tomorrow.

Dale's dad did not come home for dinner. His worried mom phoned his company to see where he was. No one answered the phone, and Dale and Mom wondered why he hadn't phoned. Dale started crying. "I want to see Daddy," he told his mom.

The next morning, Dale woke up to see his mom smiling at his bedroom door. "Last night, Daddy got called by the Air

Force Reserve. He had to fly to France right away. Do you know where France is"?

Dale shook his head.

"We'll look it up on a map," Mom said.

"Will he be home today?" Dale asked.

"No. He won't be home for a while."

"How long?"

"I don't know. When reserve pilots are called to active duty, they just have to go for as long as they are needed."

Dale didn't know what to think, but when days turned into weeks, Dale got scared even though Daddy had written several letters. After all, Daddy had told Dale that he would always come home in a day or two. Why was it taking so long? Maybe the letters were fake. Maybe Daddy was dead. Maybe Daddy had left his family.

Dale began to withdraw. He barely spoke at home. He would no longer read aloud at school and never raised his hand. His teacher told his mom he appeared to be grieving. "What has happened to him?" she asked. Dale's mom told his teacher that he missed his dad.

But Dale wouldn't tell her why he was so sad. He realized his mother did not know his dad was dead, and he did not want to tell her.

Dale's mom took Dale to the doctor, and the physician diagnosed depression. He explained to Dale that his dad was just away on a mission and would return, but Dale didn't believe him. Dale was mad at his dad for dying.

After his dad had been gone for over a month, Dale lay in bed one night with a familiar sick feeling in his stomach. Maybe if Dale asked God, God would let him go to Daddy.

Suddenly, Dale saw something glowing in the corner of his room. He sat up in his bed, and as he watched, the glow became larger and more radiant. The figure of a woman emerged, and she looked like the angels in a book he had read.

The lady moved closer to him and sat beside Dale, taking his hand in hers. "Dale, listen to me," she said. "You have been very worried about your dad, but you don't need to be afraid."

"Where is he?" Dale asked.

"He is in France, flying with the Air Force, just like your mother told you," she said. "He had to go away suddenly, and there wasn't time for him to say goodbye. I am watching over your father, Dale. I will make sure he comes home safely to you when his job is finished. You help your mother while you're waiting for him, all right?"

"Yes!" Dale exclaimed, so happy to get the good news from his heavenly visitor. The sick feeling left, and he felt light and bouncy.

The bright figure began to fade away. Dale reached out to her, but she was gone.

The next morning, Dale's mom was relieved when her son bounded down the stairs, ate three bowls of cereal, and headed off to school with a smile.

When his teacher phoned later in the day, she told his mom that Dale seemed fine. "He read a whole story to the class today. I wonder what made him change."

"I don't know," replied Dale's mom, "but I'm going to give God a very big thank you for making my little boy well and happy again."

A few weeks later, Dale's dad came home safe and sound.[18]

Angel Assures Wife She Would Hear from Her Soldier Husband, Missing in Action

Marilyn was one of many World War II wives whose husbands were fighting overseas. Marilyn's husband, Jim, was fighting in Germany. She lived in fear of getting one of those dreaded telegrams from the United States government.

As Marilyn was getting ready for work one morning, her doorbell rang. No one made social calls at that time of the day, so she went to the door with her heart pounding. A man in an immaculate uniform stood there and handed her a telegram. She tore it open and read, "We regret to inform you that your husband is missing in action."

Marilyn was stunned, especially because there was no mention of any details in the telegram. As the weeks dragged on, Marilyn dealt with her doubts and fears as best she could. One night, as she was praying for Jim, she began to cry in agony.

"Oh Lord," she prayed. "It's so hard not knowing if my husband is dead or alive. If I could just have a definite word, I think I could stand anything."

Suddenly, the room was filled with an unmistakable presence standing behind Marilyn. Marilyn was terrified and started to turn around when she heard a voice.

"Do not be afraid, and do not turn around," she was instructed.

Marilyn's fear dissolved, and a quietness enveloped her. She felt like waves of peace flowed over her, comforting her heart.

Then the voice said, "You will hear on April 13," and the angelic being was gone.

Two weeks later, on April 13, Marilyn received a postcard written in her husband's handwriting saying he was safe. He had been captured in the Battle of the Bulge and was a prisoner of war in Germany. At the end of the war, Jim returned home safely.[19]

An Angel Brings Comfort to a Grieving Father

Reverend L.W. Northrup shares his story of angel encouragement and comfort following the death of his only son, a twenty-one-year-old college student who was loved by everyone. As the family gathered to celebrate the Easter weekend one year, Rev. Northrup, his wife, and daughters were at home on Good Friday evening when the phone rang. The operator on the other line told the revered his son had been seriously injured in an accident. The family jumped in the car and raced to the hospital as fast as possible, only to hear upon arrival, "He's gone."

Gerald, their son, had been working at a church with some of his college friends when a piece of machinery crushed his head. He died during surgery at the hospital. His buddies said his last words were, "Please, Jesus, help me."

Losing a beloved son would be incredibly hard for any family. What made it so much more difficult for Rev. Northrup was his belief that his son, headed for seminary after graduation in six weeks, would one day pick up his mantle and minister far more effectively than the good reverend himself. He wrote, "The cup I drank that dark night was so bitter. The unanswered questions were so difficult to resolve."

A few months later, Rev. Northrup was on a trip to the Holy Land, fulfilling a lifelong dream. On Christmas Eve, he and his friends worshiped with an interdenominational group sponsored by the YMCA at the Shepherd's Cave near Bethlehem. Then, they split up and went their separate ways.

Rev. Northrup went back to his hotel and was hit by a wave of grief that seemed unbearable. He had never been apart from his family on Christmas before, and a deep sorrow swept over him as he felt the keen loss of his dear boy.

Christmas Day dawned bright and beautiful, and the good reverend decided to make an early morning visit to the Garden Tomb before the crowds arrived. He went to find solace for his pain and loneliness. Just as he had hoped, not a soul was there to mar his visit with his Lord and Savior.

As he stood by the open door of the tomb, he became aware of a presence standing beside him. The being was in the likeness of an angel and spoke softly, "Your son is not here. He is risen."

With those words of truth of where his beloved son was, all sorrow vanished. The tears flowed, but they were tears of joy. He left the Garden triumphantly and was able to continue the journey and experience the wonders of what he had so long anticipated.[20]

A Spiritual Mentor

Howard Storm was a professor who made it clear he wanted no part of God or any religious discussion in his college classes. If a student so much as tried to mention God, Professor Storm would take the student aside and tell him or her that such discussions were not permitted in his classroom.

On a trip to France one summer, Professor Storm developed severe abdominal pains. He was taken to a French hospital and diagnosed with a perforated stomach. The medical team in France believed he needed immediate surgery since he would not survive a trip home without undergoing the medical procedure. As Professor Storm was prepped and anesthetized, he felt himself descending into a terrible place where horrid creatures were waiting to torment him. He did not want to go with them and remembered something from his childhood— Psalm 23. He recited it and called out, asking Jesus to save him. Suddenly, in the middle of the terrifying creatures, Jesus appeared and pushed him upward toward the light. He was safe!

Slowly he recovered from the surgery and returned home a new man. He now wanted as much of God as possible in his life. He couldn't believe people did not acknowledge God and now wanted to help them know the Jesus who saved him.

He joined a church and became friends with the pastor, Reverend Bill Crawford, who tried to help him process what had happened to him. He started reading books by the monk Thomas Merton, who became a virtual mentor to him. Pastor Bill suggested they take a trip to the monastery where Merton wrote and was buried, so one bright fall day, they took off and drove to the abbey.

A monk directed them to the grave of Thomas Merton and left them alone. As Professor Storm prayed on his knees by Merton's grave, tears streamed down his face because he felt the presence of the saint so keenly. Suddenly, a young man appeared by his side and handed him a book of Merton's poems opened to a poem titled "*The Cemetery at Gethsemane.*" After he read the poem, he understood that Merton had felt the presence of the saints buried in the cemetery each time he visited.

Professor Storm handed the book back to the young man, closed his eyes, and said a brief prayer of thanks. When he opened his eyes, the young man was gone. His pastor, watching from a bench, said the man just vanished.

Later, Professor Storm was looking at some photos of Merton and found one of him in his twenties. The young Merton looked exactly like the young man in the cemetery.[21]

Summary

The stories in this chapter show us another facet of angels' ministries to humans. They are comforting and encouraging and share crucial information given to them by God. Sometimes, it only takes a gentle reminder of the truth, like the word spoken to Reverend Northrup that his son was in heaven, to lift sorrow from a downcast soul. Little Dale was a new boy after the angel assured him his dad would come home safely. And, how encouraging to learn from a taxi driver that you would win your Supreme Court case. God's special delivery angels even know what to "wear." The heavenly make-up team must have had a good time making the angel who encouraged Howard Storm look like a young Thomas Merton. Is there no limit to the talents of these heavenly allies?

Angels with Healing in Their Wings

"For a good angel will accompany him; his journey will be successful, and he will come back in good health."

Tobit 5:22

Angels can impersonate anyone. One writer has noted that next to mechanics, they impersonate doctors and nurses more frequently than anyone else. Angels show up in hospitals, doctors' offices, and bedrooms, bringing comfort, peace, and healing to people recovering from illness. It was an angel healing story from my friend Mark Newton that triggered my interest in angels. Mark is the first person I knew to share a personal encounter with angels, and I was fascinated.

Mark's Healing Story

Mark is middle-aged with four children and an excellent job in the insurance industry. About five years ago, Mark began frequently passing out for no apparent reason. His doctor ordered tests, which didn't identify the cause of his frequent blackouts. He was hospitalized for more tests. After four long days of testing, the doctors eliminated everything except for brain cancer. Mark was scheduled for testing the next morning.

The night before they were going to perform the test, Mark was overcome with fear. What would his family do if he died? How would his wife cope? Who would walk his daughters down the aisle at their weddings? Who would mentor his sons as they started out on their own? His wife and children needed him, and he desperately wanted to be there for them.

That night, a friend from church came to pray with him. The friend, in praying, asked God to pour out his fire upon Mark. After the friend left, Mark talked to his wife and children using Facetime on his phone. His wife exclaimed, "Mark, you look like you have a sunburn." Then his daughter got on the phone and repeated her mother's words

As Mark finished the conversation, he looked up and could not believe what he saw. Mighty "warrior angels" were stationed in his hospital room at both windows. He said they looked like Navy Seals on steroids—huge and ferocious beings with shields and spears, dressed in red. He whispered, "God, are these angels?"

God responded, "Yes, and two more are stationed outside your door."

Then, some "softer" angels dressed in white came and hovered around his hospital bed. The hovering angels comforted him and brought him peace. He quit worrying about the tests.

When the test results came in, everything was negative. Mark was released from the hospital. Unbeknownst to Mark, his sister, a pastor's wife, had been praying that he would have a divine encounter. The warrior and comforting angels were her answer, but a few days after his release, Mark began to question himself. Were those truly angels he had seen?

Before going to the hospital, Mark had been on a "read through the Bible in a year" program. He wanted to resume it and happened to be in the Book of Nahum. He had just about decided to skip Nahum because he figured the Old Testament prophet wouldn't have anything relevant to say to him. But something told him to go ahead and read it anyway.

When he got to Nahum 2:3, he almost dropped his Bible. The passage described God's warriors, and Mark instantly recognized the description of the warriors in his translation of Nahum. The passage accurately described the angels he had seen stationed at his hospital windows. The angels not only deepened Mark's faith but also brought healing. Mark never experienced another blackout after his release from the hospital.[22]

An Angel Doctor Appears Just in Time

My cousin, Betsy, tells a story about a hospital visit when she took her roommate, Barbara, who suffered from several debilitating diseases, to the emergency room. As they were waiting to be seen after Barbara suffered a serious attack, Barbara was given oxygen through her nose. Betsy, sitting beside her roomie, dozed off, and when the oxygen tube slipped out of Barbara's nose, she didn't know it.

All of a sudden, a small, dark-skinned physician appeared and said, "Something told me I should come and check on you." She gently placed the oxygen tube back in Barbara's nose and left.

Barbara told Betsy later that she had been hovering over her body, looking down at it before the doctor put the oxygen tube back in her nose. "And you were sleeping on the job," she chided.

When Barbara was treated and released, she and Betsy went to find the female doctor who had been so helpful to thank her. They described her to several nurses but were told by everyone they asked that no one matching that description worked there. Betsy said they had encountered an angel.[23]

Angel Appears as a Patient's Sister

A Vietnamese veteran tells the story about being released from the VA hospital in Portland, Oregon, in the late seventies. As he and a friend walked in front of the hospital after his release, a girl approached them. She was blonde and had been crying. She said, "My brother is dying in this hospital. He's not going to be here for too long!" She asked the veteran and his friend to go and pray for her brother, explaining he wasn't a Christian. She gave them his room number. The two men went in to see this man the girl had asked them to pray for.

The brother had leukemia and throat cancer, and doctors had just finished an operation on him. He was in bad shape. The doctor came in, and as he turned to face the two friends who had come to pray, he said the patient would probably pass away before morning.

A few minutes later, a pastor came in and asked the patient if he would like to be saved. The brother nodded yes, and the pastor led the man to Christ.

After praying for this man, the Vietnamese vet and his friend left but returned the next morning to see how he was doing. They saw that his bed was clean and the mattress rolled up. When they asked the staff if he was still alive, someone said, "Yes, but he's been transferred from here."

Three months later, the Vietnamese vet was at the same hospital and ran into the brother for whom they had prayed a few months earlier. The vet was surprised to see that the former patient was passing out flyers for the chaplain's office. The brother recognized the vet, approached him, and thanked him for his care. The Vietnamese vet said, "Well, this girl outside of the hospital came out of nowhere and she asked us to come up and pray for you, her brother."

Suddenly, the former patient's face went white. He dropped everything he had in his hands and exclaimed, "My sister is dead! She was killed three years ago in a car accident." He pulled out his wallet to show them a picture, and it was the same girl. No question. She was even wearing the same clothes as in the picture. The vet was stunned. He had never experienced anything like that before, and it brought a whole new meaning to his faith and belief.

These creative angles can even appear as deceased family members, which one did in this case.[24]

An Angel Appearing as a Tramp

Marian Ash tells the story of the unlikely angel who came to his house in the middle of the Depression during a winter snowstorm. Marion said that many homeless people came to their home during this dark time and his mother always fed them. Her favorite Bible verse was Hebrews 13:2, "Do not neglect to show hospitality to strangers, for by doing that some have entertained angels without knowing it."

At the time of this particular visit, Marion was a young boy and had a baby sister, Lucy, who was ill with a high fever. The town doctor was sick and could not get over to give the baby any relief or medicine. His mother continuously put cold cloths on her head to try to get the fever down but was getting worried when the fever did not break. His dad said taking her to the local hospital would be risky since the roads were covered with deep snow.

They saw an old man struggling up the lane leading to their house as they tried to decide what to do. He knocked, and Marion saw his dad's shocked expression. Marion's dad was generally opposed to having strangers in his home. This man had a thick stocking cap pulled over his ears, and his long beard was covered in snowflakes. His topcoat was thin and ragged, and he wasn't wearing gloves. In one hand, his fingers clutched a small bag containing all his worldly possessions.

"Could you spare an old man a cup of tea and a bite to eat?" he asked in a weak, pleading voice. "I stopped at the house up the road, but no one answered. I guess no one was home."

Marion's dad was about to send him away, but his mother immediately said, "Let him in, Frank. He's welcome to stay for lunch."

The old man smiled and said, "God bless you."

Marion's dad helped him out of his topcoat and settled by the fire. On the way to his seat, he passed by the crib where baby Lucy was sleeping. Marion's mother explained that her baby was very sick, and the doctor was not able to come over. The old man said, "She has a burning fever, doesn't she?" He put his wrinkled hand lightly on her tiny fingers.

Marion's mom hurried off to prepare lunch, and Dad asked the old man where he was headed. "Alabama," he said. Dad was amazed because Alabama was hundreds of miles from where they were.

Marion's mom worked over the stove cooking and pulled out a jar of her canned beets, the very ones that won her a first-place blue ribbon at the state fair. When Dad protested and said she should save them for a special occasion, Mom told him this was a special occasion. Dad continued grumbling and said he hoped Mom would be paid for all of her trouble someday. "Oh, I will," Mom exclaimed, and she had never said anything so emphatically before.

When lunch was ready the old man came to the table and softly asked if he might say a blessing over the food. Mom nodded yes, and he proceeded, thanking God for the food and the gracious family who took him in and asking God to lay his healing hand upon their baby girl.

The old man kept eating and had several helpings of the red beets, eating them until they were all gone. He then told Mom he had never tasted such good beets.

Shortly after finishing his lunch, the old man said he had to be going. He wanted to make it to the next village before sundown. Mom left the table and went to the back room. When she returned, she had one of Dad's discarded topcoats and a pair of gloves. She handed them to the old man and said they would like him to have them.

He took the offered gifts, expressing thanks for them and saying God would surely bless them for it. As he left, he stopped by Lucy's crib and laid his hand on her forehead. The family saw him praying quietly, with just his lips moving.

On the porch, he turned to thank the family with tears in his eyes. "Goodbye, dear friends. I'll not be passing this way again. May God's richest blessings be on you." The family stood on the porch until the snow obscured the old man from view.

Mom turned to go back into the house. "Lucy!" she cried. Marion and his dad came running in. Lucy was sitting up in her bed. Her fever was gone. Mom lifted the baby from her crib, and Marion said she was happier than he had ever seen her. Marion said two miracles occurred that day. Lucy was healed and Dad had a complete change of heart about entertaining the strangers that came to their door. He now saw why Mom was always ready and willing to help them—indeed, they could be angels.[25]

Angel Delivers Instructions to Save Charge from Poison

L.W. Northrup went all over the world preaching the gospel to countries where standards of cleanliness were not up to what he was used to. On one occasion he was traveling with a group in Athens, Greece. His sister, a nurse, was with him, and she had insisted that he take along some over-the-counter medications for digestive issues that might arise.

It so happened that several people on the tour had stomach problems. When they learned that L.W. had meds, they made their needs known, and he graciously gave them what he had. One day, however, en route to Corinth, they stopped at a restaurant no one had recommended. It looked fine, but a few hours after lunch, L.W. began to feel sick. At first, he thought it would pass, but as time wore on, he felt worse and worse. He thought he had been poisoned.

He was normally a very healthy person, so when severe digestive problems arose, he could only conclude the worst.

Maybe someone was trying to stop him from preaching the gospel message. He didn't know.

He canceled his service for the evening in Athens since none of his efforts to find relief were successful. All of his medications had been given to his fellow travelers. Adding to his agony was the fact that no one else seemed to be sick this time. The rest of his group was out sightseeing, leaving him alone.

He thought he was dying thousands of miles away from home—alone, no less, away from his tour group. L.W. knew that a voice he calls his angel had spoken to him many times in the past, and he had been grateful. When he heard that voice again saying, "Put your fingers together in a point and shove them down your throat as far as you can," he quickly complied.

He put his fingers down so far into his esophagus he thought he would touch his stomach and vomited up an ugly black mass. He described it as a lump of coal, nothing like one normally experiences from a simple upset stomach.

Delivered from the poisonous mass, he fell on the floor—weak but alive. He crawled into his bed and slept. Thanks to the good advice from his angel, he was healed and saved. L.W. also believed he received some kind of immunity from the experience. In trips following this visit to Athens, he never again became ill whether eating food prepared by natives or in restaurants. While others in his group succumbed, he did not and seemed to have been granted permanent immunity to native foods.[26]

Angel Doctor Comforts Christian-to-Be

Martha lost her husband to cancer and was coping as best she could with four small children. When she became ill, she feared the worst—that she, too, had cancer.

She asked her neighbor, a nurse, for a recommendation of a good doctor, and Mavis, the neighbor, recommended Dr. Everhart. Martha made the appointment and went to the doctor's office, dreading whatever he might find. She didn't know what her children would do without a father or mother.

After she had checked in with the receptionist, she noticed a doctor heading toward her in the reception area. He greeted her and asked her how she was doing. Although Martha wanted to share her true feelings, she said the expected thing, "I'm all right, I guess."

The nurse showed her into an examining room, and Martha changed into the hospital gown and lay on the table waiting for Dr. Everhart. After a few minutes, the door opened, and the doctor who had previously greeted her came over and gently put his hand on hers, saying, "When I saw you in the waiting room, I sensed you were frightened. Would you like to tell me about it?" Martha said she had never heard a kinder voice.

Without hesitation, Martha poured out her frustrations and anxieties of the past two years since her husband had died. When she paused long enough to catch her breath, the doctor said, "I'm here to let you know I care. This time will pass and you will have plenty of sunny days ahead. Try not to worry so much."

He then told her he would see her later and left the room. Shortly thereafter, Dr. Everhart came in and began the dreaded examination. "Good news!" he said upon completing the exam. "There's nothing wrong with you that good medicine won't fix."

Martha fairly floated home that day, not only because of the good diagnosis but also because someone had taken the time to listen to her and to care. When she arrived at her house, she saw Mavis in her yard and went over to share the good news. "Mavis, I'm going to be fine. Thank you for referring me to Dr. Everhart. But who was that other doctor in his office? He was so kind to me. He listened to every concern of my heart and assured me things would get better."

Mavis looked confused. "There is no other doctor in that office. Dr. Everhart is the only one, and I have heard him say it would stay that way."

Martha was perplexed until she ran into another friend, Lillian, a few days later and shared her experience. Lillian immediately said, "My dear, you have had an encounter with an angel. God sends angels to comfort us when we are in distress."

Martha looked at Lillian in astonishment and asked, "Why would God send an angel to me? I've never done anything but run away from God."

Lillian casually explained, "They are sent to those who are to inherit salvation to bring help and comfort."

Martha listened and then, because she knew Lillian taught a weekly Bible study, asked if she might attend. Lillian assured her she would be most welcome and told her where and when the group met.

For four years, Martha faithfully attended Lillian's Bible study. She learned who God is, that he loves her, and that Jesus died for her sins. She learned what being saved meant and decided to accept Jesus as her savior and start life on a new path. Her life began to show evidence of her relationship with Christ as she learned more and more and spent time in God's Word and talking to God.

As Martha thought about how she had come to this new life God had given her, she remembered the angel doctor who had been so kind to her when she was afraid of leaving her children alone. She realized he was the one who set the chain of events in motion, leading to her eternal salvation. Indeed, the angel was sent to her because God knew she would become one of his children through Jesus Christ.[27]

Summary

Why do angels appear to some who are sick but not all? We don't know, but we do know that some angels are prayed in (like the ones who came to Mark Newton, prayed in by his sister), and some are sent to those who are to inherit salvation.[28] My guess is that many angels are sent to those who are sick and are never identified as angels on this side of heaven. Angels seem to prefer working *incognito* whenever possible. They may well be doing their work in every hospital and every facility where sick people are recovering without anyone ever knowing of their divine status.

Heaven's Ushers

"Angels in the room, when you run your final race. They will carry you to heaven, there to see your savior's face."

Bill and Gloria Gaither

A reader of Dr. Billy Graham's syndicated column posed the following question: "When we die, does an angel accompany us into heaven? I've heard this all my life, but is it really true? How do we know?" Signed Mrs. P.F.

Dr. Graham answers Mrs. P.F. that, indeed, the Bible indicates that when a believer dies, angels will escort that believer safely to heaven. Jesus confirmed this in one of his parables about two very different men. One was rich and uncaring, living only for himself. He died and received what he deserved: a life separated from God. The other, a poor beggar who had faith in God and his promises, was ushered by the angel safely into God's presence at his dying moment.[29]

Dr. Graham notes that if angels safeguard us on planet Earth ("For he will command his angels concerning you to guard you in all your ways." Psalm 91:11), can't they also be trusted to take us to heaven safely?[30]

Another pastor, Charles B. Bell, in his book *Angelic Beings, Their Nature and Ministry*, writes, "Angels gather round the dying beds of believers, waiting until the spirit be set free, that they may bear their charge with songs to its Father's home. Which of us has not heard of saints who in their last moments had visions of angels—glimpses of bright faces, and caught strains of richest music, just as heaven was opening its doors to let them in?...Blessed indeed are they for whom death, having lost its sting, is lightened by angel-presences and angel whispers..."[31]

Pastors and hospice nurses who minister to dying patients often report stories of those to whom they've ministered, seeing angels and hearing heavenly music right before the individual passes away.

A Young Mom Describing Angels to Her Children

One nurse, Joy, who attended many dying persons, was especially concerned about her patient, a thirty-five-year-old mother of two. Joy, along with the children, aged six and nine, were with their mother in her dying moments. Just before she died, she described to her children the angels who had come to escort her into the presence of her Lord and Savior. She told her children the angels were cheerful, healthy-looking young angels holding her hands and telling her how excited God was to have her come home.

She said they described her new home in heaven where the floors never needed waxing and that Jesus would meet her there at the front door. She also told them there was a choir for her to sing with in heaven, and she had a front-row seat.

Then she explained that she made the angels promise to watch over both of them and bring them to Jesus. With that, she gently passed away.

Joy said it was the most positive approach to helping children cope with death she had ever witnessed.[32]

A Devoted Son Witnesses an Angel Escorting His Dad Home

Bill deeply loved his dad. Although his dad was in his late eighties, Bill knew he would feel a sense of deep loss when he was gone, and his dad was close to death. When the hospital called late one night, Bill quickly made his way to his father's bedside. He was grief-stricken as he looked at his dad's gentle face, remembering the day when he had been a vibrant, energetic doctor who healed bodies and comforted souls. As Bill sat beside his dad, his father suddenly opened his eyes and said in a clear, strong voice, "Bill, I hear the most beautiful choir of angels singing." And then, Bill saw an angel standing beside the bed between him and his father who filled the room with an intense feeling of love and peace that Bill had never before experienced. Bill looked at his dad and saw his face was as radiant and glowing as the angel's. After a few moments, Bill's dad breathed his last breath. Bill sat quietly in the room and continued to feel the peace and love that had accompanied the angel, grateful he had been given a special gift of a glimpse into eternity.[33]

Although the deathbed appearances of angels vary, they all seem to provide comfort and encouragement for the person transitioning from mortal life to eternal life and for close family and friends as well. Some see angels in physical form and marvel at their radiant beauty; some hear heavenly music; some see gardens and flowers; some glimpse heaven; some encounter a comforting light; and some see sparkles. Sometimes, loved ones with the dying also see angels, and sometimes not.

A client of mine whose wife was nearing the end of her life from a prolonged illness told her husband that Jesus was in the room with them right before she died. She asked him to get a chair for Jesus to sit in. The husband did not see Jesus, but he could tell the vision was very real to his dying wife.

While each experience is tailor-made for the individual saint and his or her family, all assure us we are not alone at death. The angels comfort, assure, and escort us to our heavenly home.

Angel Coming to the Hospital Room to Take a Mother Home

Mary Louise Young had been struggling all day with her breathing and lay unconscious in her hospital bed. Her daughter, Betty Powell, sat beside her, and her son, John Young, and her granddaughter, Kathy Powell, kept vigil with Betty. All of a sudden, Mary Louise's eyes opened wide, and as Betty explained it, she clearly saw something remarkable. Almost immediately after, Mary Louise stopped breathing. She was gone.

A nurse came in and verified Mary Louise's death, telling the family to take their time and stay in the room as long as they wanted to. The nurse said she would place a sign on the door so no one would bother them.

About ten minutes after the nurse left, a man walked in without knocking. He wore white except for gold trim around his neck, and Betty said he was almost dazzling. He went to the foot of Mary Louise's bed, looked at each of the three family members, and said, "It is over." He smiled and then turned around and left the room as suddenly as he had come in.

John followed him out to ask who he was, but as soon as he reached the hallway, the man was nowhere in sight. John then went to the nurse's station and asked about him. The nurses were puzzled and told John no one fitting that description worked there. When John described his outfit, they said no hospital uniform looked like that.

As Betty, John, and Kathy reflected on the visit from the stranger, they concluded he had to be an angel sent to take their mother and grandmother home to heaven.[34]

Angels Appearing as Stars

Shari Abbott tells the story of her devout mother's death on a wintery night in Michigan. Shari's brother, a nonbeliever, was with their mom at the hospital. Shari had been called but lived hours away and could not get to the hospital due to the weather knocking out a bridge.

Her brother watched as his mother's breath became more and more labored. Finally, she took her last breath, and at that moment, he saw what he described as sparkles descending up to the ceiling of the hospital room.

Shari notes that angels have appeared to look like stars in the Bible (Revelation 1:20 and 12:4). She believes the sparkles were a sign to her brother that life after death is real and an answer to her mother's prayers for his salvation, inviting him to turn and believe in God and his promises.[35]

Light and Sweet Aromas

Robin Morrison shares the story of her best friend's diagnosis of terminal brain cancer, requiring brain surgery, chemo, and radiation therapies. Although the surgery placed severe limitations on his speech, when Robin would go and visit with CDs and a player, he was able to sing praise songs with her as though he was in perfect health.

Robin said they sometimes had a sense of others being with them as they worshiped. When this happened, the light level in the room would become brighter, and they smelled a sweet aroma. During these times, they knew they were part of another realm, one of heavenly worship with the angels.

During the friend's illness, Robin had a dream. She was in a great assembly of people worshiping God. Angels were everywhere playing instruments, standing guard, and offering up incense. Robin's friend stood beside her, singing at the top of his lungs. He was strong, full of life, and so happy. He looked at Robin and said, "I'm outta here."

Robin became aware of some large, gentle, yet powerful hands resting on her shoulders, reassuring her as she watched her friend being escorted to heaven by angels.

A phone call woke Robin up. Her friend had just gone to be with his Lord that very morning.[36]

Comfort to a Prayer Warrior

H.T. had been praying for the healing of a twelve-year-old boy at her church who was suffering from terminal leukemia. The pastor, however, was praying and encouraging others to pray that the boy would die quickly so he wouldn't suffer. H.T.

thought this was wrong and asked the pastor to pray for healing instead. The pastor explained the boy was terminal and a quick death would end his pain.

Unconvinced, H.T. continued to fast and pray for the boy's healing. On the fourth morning of her fast, news came that the boy had died. H.T. was deeply saddened but believed God's will had prevailed.

After the funeral, H.T. found it difficult to stop thinking about the boy. Her energy had been depleted, and she felt apprehensive. Walking into her kitchen she was shocked to see a "giant, radiating, pure, intense, golden light" which she knew to be an angel.

The angel communicated a message to her without speaking a word. Beside the angel was the boy who had just died. The angel nudged him, and with some reluctance, the boy said, "Thank you." The angel gently drew the boy back into the light and disappeared.

As H.T. contemplated what she had just seen, she felt herself being lifted and carried into the living room, where her Bible lay open on the end table next to the couch. She looked down and read, "He said to him, 'If they do not listen to Moses and the prophets, neither will be they be convinced even if someone rises from the dead.'"[37] A great peace washed over her as she realized that her fasting and prayers for the twelve-year-old boy had been answered—he was whole and well in heaven.[38]

Summary

How comforting to know we will not be alone as we move out of our earthly bodies and into the mansions Jesus has promised us. Whether our loved ones see the angels or not, they are there, escorting us and warding off evil spirits trying to interfere. No wonder David wrote, "Even though I walk through the darkest valley, I fear no evil; for you are with me...."[39]

Each journey is tailor-made by the Creator of the universe. He sends his angels to minister comfort, peace, and assurance to the departing saint and, sometimes, to their family and close friends. Angels show up when we need them, and when we face the great unknown—death—we need them to usher us into our permanent heavenly homes.

Angels and Travelers

"... The Lord, before whom I walk, will send his angel with you and make your way successful...."

Genesis 24:40

Many people take advantage of AAA (American Automobile Association) when traveling. AAA provides help when vehicles break down, discounts at hotels and restaurants, and travel planning. However, there is another travel organization dubbed STAR, by authors Lonnie Melashenko and Timothy Crosby, that helps travelers. STAR stands for Seraphic Travelers Aid Resources, God's appointed angel travel agency.

When God's children head out on journeys, he knows they will lack resources normally available to them and might need some extra help. Their cars might break down, they might need help with bicycles or motorcycles, small watercraft can present problems, and airplanes can also encounter mechanical issues while airborne.

STAR is the oldest of all travel agencies. When Abraham sent his servant on a journey to find a wife for his son Issac, he told him, "...The Lord, before whom I walk, will send his angel with you and make your way successful...."[40] In Exodus 23:20, God tells Moses, "I am going to send an angel in front of you, to guard you on the way and to bring you to the place I have prepared."

Travel has greatly increased since the time of Abraham and Moses, so it's no surprise STAR is busier today than ever. Unlike AAA, you don't need to sign up with STAR ahead of time to take advantage of their services.

Angels on the Interstate

I want to share my personal angel travel story to kick off the stories in this chapter. Although I did not actually see the angel or the angels involved, there is no way what happened could have occurred without divine intervention protecting me and everyone else involved.

About twenty years ago, one August afternoon, I was driving from north Georgia to Atlanta on I-85. I had just left friends, and we had enjoyed a delicious buffet lunch where I had eaten way too much. As I was driving, I began feeling drowsy, but I turned up the air conditioning and radio and slapped my face a few times to wake up. I thought that would take care of my problem.

All of a sudden, I felt violent jolting. I realized I was in the grassy median between the north and south lanes of I-85. Before I could do anything, my car bounced back on I-85 and started spinning around. By that time, I knew I had gone to sleep at the wheel and cried out, "Jesus, help me!"

The car was headed across the interstate toward some trees on my right-hand side. I steered it away from them, causing it to go into another spin. *This is not safe. Someone could hit me.*

All of a sudden, my car came to a stop, facing the oncoming traffic. As I looked up, I saw the traffic STOPPED, WATCHING THE SHOW. Four cars abreast stopped, and not one of them was even involved in so much as a fender bender.

When I saw I was safe, I turned the car around and pulled over to the side of the interstate. Several people jumped out of their cars and ran up to ask me if I was okay. I told them I had fallen asleep at the wheel but was all right. One of the guys said, "Stay right here. I'll call the police to come help you."

That suited me fine. I was too shaken up to go anywhere.

After a few minutes, a nice police officer arrived. I told him what had happened, and he said he would help me get to the nearest exit so I could get something to revive me. The officer led me to a convenience store and said, "Get a soda and stay here until you feel rested." He then drove off.

I don't know how long I stayed at the convenience store. I was trying to process what had happened. I knew my life had been miraculously spared. And God, in his goodness, had protected everyone else involved as well. I knew it was not humanly possible for all of those cars to be stopped on I-85, watching while I regained control of my car. I like to think some of them were praying for me, and I believe they were. I would have been praying if I had witnessed such a spectacle.

As I continued to process the experience, knowing God was involved, I came to believe it was his agents, the angels, who miraculously stopped the cars on I-85, giving me time to regain control and get to safety. Think about it: cars on I-85 are going 70 mph (if they're obeying the speed limit). Could they all stop safely and simultaneously to allow for a car in trouble? It just doesn't seem possible to me. Angels had to have been involved.

Angel Prepares Motorcyclist for Danger

I recently shared this writing project with my hairdresser. He said, "I have a story for you."

"Please tell me," I said.

"I was nineteen, living in California. I had a motorcycle and loved to take it out to go and see my friends. At that time, there were no helmet laws in California. (As of January 1, 1992, California enacted a law requiring all motorcyclists to wear helmets.)

"One day, I went out to ride my motorcycle without my helmet. Something told me to put my helmet on, but I ignored it. The closer I got to the motorcycle, the stronger this voice in my head became. *Put on your helmet*. Finally, as I got right up to the bike, ready to get on it, the voice was so strong and forceful, I remember actually yelling to it, 'All right, all right!' I went back to the house, got my helmet, and put it on.

"I jumped on my motorcycle and pulled out onto a main artery in the city, and probably hadn't gone two miles before a drunk driver cut across my path, making a collision with him unavoidable. I flew over the front of my motorcycle head first, crashing into a window of his car, shattering the glass. When I was pulled from the wreck, I was told if I hadn't been wearing my helmet, I would've been killed. I know my angel warned me and kept pestering me until I got that helmet on my head.[41]

Angel Mechanics

We are all thankful for our earthly mechanics who get our cars running and keep them in shape. As good as they are, they are nothing compared to God's army of angel mechanics who can fix cars on the spot, sometimes with just a touch!

Ruby S. and a friend were traveling from Palm Beach to Orlando, Florida when their car stopped near the Sebastian Inlet and wouldn't start. They didn't know what to do. As they sat there pondering their options, a young man came up on a motorcycle and asked if they needed help. They explained their dilemma and told him they needed a good mechanic.

The young man went back to his motorcycle and pulled out a piece of wire from his bag. He lifted the hood of their car and did something with it, telling the ladies that now their car would start. However, he warned, "Don't stop until you get to your destination because it won't start again until it is permanently fixed."

Ruby started the car and turned to thank the young man, but no one was there. They also realized they didn't hear the sound of a motorcycle leaving the scene. They then knew that one of God's angel mechanics had taken care of them.[42]

Another angel mechanic took care of Norma L. on a very dark night as she and her eleven-year-old daughter were traveling back from a trip to visit her mother-in-law. All of a sudden, their headlights went out. They were on a major highway with cars whizzing by.

Norma turned on her right turn signal, hoping to find a suitable exit quickly. As cars continued to pass them at dizzying speeds, she prayed for guidance and protection. After about fifteen minutes of blind driving, she spotted a gas station. Driving carefully so she would not drive into a ditch, she made it to the gas station, breathing a prayer of thanksgiving.

Right away, a young man dressed in overalls with a gasoline brand on the uniform came toward her and asked, "May I help you?"

"Certainly!" Norma exclaimed. "Our headlights went out, and we've been driving in the dark."

The man did not say anything but placed both hands on the hood of her Jeep, and immediately, the lights came to life, bright and glowing. That was it—just a laying on of the hands!

"Thank you, thank you," said Norma. "How much do we owe you?"

"Nothing," he said. Again, Norma thanked him and drove around the gas station to get back on the highway.

As Norma rounded the building, she saw an older man sitting in the office, reading a newspaper. She stopped and went in to tell him. "Sir, we were in a predicament and your nice young assistant was so kind to help us that I wanted to thank you too."

The man looked surprised and replied, "Sorry, but I don't have any assistants. I work here alone."

Norma protested, "But we saw him. He helped us."

"No, ladies, I am here alone."

Norma then knew God had sent an angel to fix her headlights, which never again failed her.[43]

An Angel Puts on the Brakes

Angels can start cars, and they can stop them. Nancy Spence of Chesterfield, Missouri, tells the story of driving toward a busy intersection. She was alone on the highway and could tell that the light at the intersection, then red, was about to change. She did not slow down or prepare to stop.

As she got close to the intersection, the light was green. Her car suddenly stopped. The radio went off, and the power steering was gone. However, it wasn't a jerky stop. It was "very soft."

Nancy looked down to see if any of the gauges were lit up to tell her what was wrong. None of them were lit. As she looked back up at the intersection, she saw a car speeding across the intersection with two police cars chasing it. They were there at the same moment she would have been in the intersection if her car had not suddenly stopped. Had she continued into the intersection, all three cars would have broadsided her.

The minute the second police car cleared the intersection, all the power came back on in Nancy's car. The radio blasted music, the air conditioning system sent cool air into the vehicle, and the car started moving without Nancy having to put her foot on the gas. As soon as she got through the intersection, she pulled over to the side of the road because she was shaking. She thanked God for saving her life, realizing if her car had not stopped, she would have been in an accident that likely would have been fatal.[44]

Angels in the Air

When airplanes get into trouble, the consequences can be catastrophic. Airplanes are high above solid ground, and if the pilot is unable to get the plane safely down, it can crash, killing everyone on board. STAR is even more important with air travel.

Ronald Bisset, who had a private pilot's license, owned a two-seater known as a taildragger that needed care and concentration when taking off and landing.

One day, he decided to take his plane up and invited an elderly gentleman who had never flown to go with him. He flew the neighbor around his homestead and other local spots and then headed back to his landing strip, which was a lane set in the middle of a wheat field. As they approached the landing spot, Ronald was shocked to see that the wind sock now indicated a dramatic change in wind direction and strength. The angle and lift of the windsock made a safe landing look doubtful, but he decided to give it a try anyway.

The approach started well, but then the wind gusted, and he felt the plane veering to the left as they grazed the wheat stalks. This caused the plane to decelerate. He reached with his right hand to close the throttle. He intended to pull back on the stick with his left hand. He hoped this would keep them from cartwheeling tail over the nose on landing.

As he went to push the throttle, he felt a hand come over the top of his right hand and pull the throttle open to full power. At the same time, another hand came over his left hand and pushed the control stick forward so that the plane went into a nose-down mode. The result of these maneuvers was that they broke out of the wheat as if they had been catapulted off the deck of an aircraft carrier.

Whoever was in control banked the plane sharply and then leveled it off to start climbing. At about a hundred feet and climbing on a straight path, he felt the other hands letting go of his and giving him back control. Ronald knew angels had been flying his plane.

Ronald looked over at his elderly passenger, who appeared unfazed by the experience. When Ronald questioned him, he simply replied, "It were quite thrillin'!"[45]

Another story of an angel taking over for a pilot comes from Eric Boyce, a helicopter bush pilot. Eric was working with surveyors in the wilderness area around Yellowstone

National Park. On one assignment, he landed to pick up a crew and fly them back to town. He radioed the crew to hurry because a rain shower was coming down the valley. The guys hurried to get in, and Eric took off. He accelerated to cruising altitude and then set up a slow descent into town.

About two minutes after takeoff, the helicopter began to shake. Eric wiggled the control stick, which usually stopped the shaking. About fifteen seconds later, it started again. Eric wiggled it again, but this time it didn't stop. Then, it started getting worse and worse. The helicopter started shaking violently, and the control stick was following the vibration, moving around in a big triangular pattern. Eric was petrified. The whole helicopter body started shaking and the crew was moaning and screaming. In addition to the shaking, the helicopter was making a terrible racket.

Eric knew he couldn't make an emergency landing because they were over a really windy creek with huge boulders "the size of Volkswagens." He started to get a bad case of tunnel vision, losing reference. He said a prayer and then said, "Everything is going to be okay!"

Eric reported that it seemed like time stopped. He heard the resonance of the helicopter change, meaning they were getting closer to the ground. He started pulling back on the stick. People were still screaming. Eric couldn't see at all but the helicopter flew from the point where he lost visual reference to a flat field about five miles away. It turned about thirty degrees and lined up with the most perfectly flat spot in Wyoming. The stick was still going around in a triangular pattern.

Eric remembers feeling an impact and then losing consciousness. The helicopter flipped upside down and flew about sixty feet, landing upside down. It caught on fire, and everyone got out except Eric. He was still upside down, hanging in his seat and struggling with his seat belt.

When the crew realized Eric was still in the helicopter, two of them came back and got him out just in time. The helicopter was destroyed, turning into a pile of charred rubble.

Eric says he knows he did not fly the helicopter from the time he lost consciousness. He couldn't have. He knows an angel flew it for him. All six passengers and Eric walked away. Only Eric had a minor injury to his chin, which hit the panel when he blacked out, causing a gash. He says when he got centered, prayed, and said, "Everything is going to be okay," he surrendered. It was like he said, "Okay, God, it's all yours. Take over." God sent an angel to get them all safely home.[46]

Angel Body Guards in a Dangerous Place

In his book, *Serving the Servants*, Dr. Ray Knighton, founder of MAP International, a worldwide ministry providing medicine and health supplies for those in need (most of whom are in third-world countries), tells the story of a trip he made to Pakistan to go to a meeting with missionary physicians.

He had to take a midnight train to his destination. Ray didn't speak the language and wondered how he would know when he arrived at Taxila, his destination. Ray decided to pretend he was the conductor and yell "Taxila" at each destination until some people got up to get off. His conductor routine proved successful. When he yelled "Taxila" and people stood to exit, he followed them off the train. It was one a.m. when Ray finally made it off the train, and to his dismay, he realized he was the only one left without someone to pick him up at the train station.

As Ray tried to figure out what to do (not knowing how to get to his destination at the hospital), three ominous figures came toward him—turbaned men with flowing robes and hard-looking, bearded faces. Ray stammered, "Taxila, Christian hospital, Christy."

To Ray's surprise, one of them spoke to him in English, "Yes, I know Dr. Christy," he said. "I'll take you there."

The man explained they were going to work at a cement factory next door to the hospital. Ray was surprised when they grabbed his luggage and hoisted it on their shoulders. Ray thought he was going to end up with a dagger in his back, but he had no choice but to follow the men, keeping up as best as he could, muddy road and all.

When they arrived at the hospital, the guard left to find Dr. Christy. Dr. Christy came to the area where Ray was waiting and said, "Ray, what are you doing here this time of the night? That road from the train station is the most dangerous in the country. It's a wonder you got here alive."

Ray turned to introduce the three men who had escorted him, but no one was there. When he told Dr. Christy one of them spoke excellent English, Dr. Christy said, "That's impossible. I am the cement factory physician, and not one of them speaks English that well."

When Ray shared his experience with a Christian doctor in the States, the doctor said, "Ray, those were guardian angels. They don't go around in white robes, you know. They are always dressed like the people around them."[47]

Summary

Psalm 91:11 says, "For he will command his angels concerning you to guard you in all your ways." Whatever mode of transportation we choose: walking, motor vehicles, bicycles, watercraft of various forms, airplanes, and even spaceships, we can ask for STAR protection. As the American Express card advertisement says, "Don't leave home without it."

Angels and Children

"Take care that you do not despise one of these little ones; for, I tell you, in heaven their angels continually see the face of my Father in heaven."

Matthew 18:10

Because angels show up at times when we are physically or emotionally vulnerable, it's no surprise there are multiple recorded incidents of angels appearing to save the lives of little ones who may not understand the consequences of their actions or the dangers they have encountered. When we are young, even through our teen years, we need special protection.

Children also seem to have a greater ability to see angels than adults. When an angel appears, sometimes only a child can see the glorious being. Perhaps this is because children have more recently come from the unseen spiritual realm where angels reside. Even when a child has never been told about angels, he or she knows who and what they are when they enter his or her world.

Angels deliver children from injury and death, warn them of dangerous situations, and comfort them when they are emotionally distraught. They can be invisible, but through an unseen force, they provide deliverance from danger. Sometimes, they show up as a human being who comes just in time to help. They may appear as a comforting light or even as an animal.

Because angels are spirits, they can assume any form they need to assume. Often, the deliverance is so ordinary it hardly seems angelic, but because the disguised angelic being just miraculously disappears right after the rescue, the people involved know it was an angel.

A Force

In 1980, a murderer of children was loose in the Atlanta, Georgia, metro area. More than twenty children and young adults would be dead at his hands before he was caught, convicted, and sent to jail.

Curfews were imposed, police patrols in neighborhoods increased, and parents warned their children to avoid all strangers.

One afternoon, an Atlanta seven-year-old named Tabitha was playing outside with her friend, Amanda. A large pea-green automobile pulled up to the curb, and the driver said to the girls, "I've got some cute puppies to find homes for, girls. Want to see them?"

Both girls started toward the car, but then Tabitha paused, remembering her mom's warning. Amanda, however, trotted right up to the vehicle when the man suddenly reached through the window and grabbed her.

Tabitha ran and caught Amanda around her waist, trying desperately to free her from his grasp. She pulled with every ounce of strength she had but she felt herself losing ground, being lifted up and through the window. Tabitha's mom had taught her to pray, so Tabitha screamed, "God send help! We don't want to die." By that time, Tabitha's feet were barely touching the ground.

Suddenly, Tabitha felt someone's arms around her waist, pulling hard from behind. The force was so great that both girls went flying backward and landed several feet from the street on the grass. The car sped away. Tabitha turned around to thank her rescuer, but no one was there. She knew it had been an angel.[48]

Angel of Warning

Brian, a Midwestern teenager, enjoyed swimming and diving with his friends in his friend's swimming pool.

One summer evening, Brian had a date with a girl in a nearby town. As he drove home that night, he noticed clouds had blocked out the moon and stars, and dense darkness encompassed the entire countryside. Before going home, he decided to drop by his friend's house for a midnight swim. Everyone was in bed, but he tiptoed up to the diving board, climbed up, and stood poised and ready to dive. As he looked into the midnight blackness, he saw what seemed to be a gleaming, brilliant glow in the shape of a cross. He also saw what appeared to be a glimmering angel stretched out below. He slowly climbed down the ladder, walked to the edge of the pool, knelt, and took a closer look. Instantly, the glow and the angel were gone, and Brian found himself looking into a swimming pool without a drop of water in it. The next day, he discovered that his friend's parents had drained the pool to clean it. Brian knows for sure that the angel came to warm him and save his life.[49]

Dancing Angels

Grandma was watching three-year-old Erik while his parents were on vacation. Erik woke up one morning, telling her his ears hurt. He had a fever and ached all over. Grandma called the doctor but couldn't get an appointment until seven in the evening. Erik was crying and wanted Grandma to hold him.

Later in the morning, Grandma put Erik on the rug with some toys, hoping they would take his mind off his pain. Then she went into the bedroom to pray, asking God to send his angels to entertain Erik.

After a little while, Erik came running to Grandma, saying, "Grandma! Grandma! Come and see the angels." He told her five angels were dancing and wearing green dresses.

No one had ever told Erik about angels before. As people questioned him later, he never changed his story. He knew what he had seen.

When Erik got to the doctor, the doctor confirmed an ear infection, but all of the pain had left with the dancing angels.[50]

Angel Comforts a Boy Whose Dad Left the Family

Judith MacNutt tells this story of how a young boy, Timmy, was comforted by an angel in his emotional distress.

Timmy, aged six, and his mom came to a healing service the MacNutts were hosting and came forward for prayer during this service. Timmy's mom, heartbroken, was recently divorced from her husband of ten years. Her deepest concern was for her young son.

Since the divorce, Timmy had withdrawn more and more and was showing symptoms of depression. He missed his dad, and he thought he was responsible for the breakup.

As Judith and her husband laid hands on Timmy and prayed, he began to cry. Something drew Judith's attention to the ceiling, and as she looked up, there sitting on the rafter high above the cross was an angel. A brilliant white light surrounded him, and his garment was shining. Judith thinks he was also praying for Timmy.

After the prayer, Timmy and his mom returned to their seats, and Judith noticed Timmy continued to look up at the ceiling. Judith excused herself from the healing line and slipped into the seat beside Timmy. She asked him what he saw.

"I see a large man sitting on a rafter," he said. Judith told him he was seeing an angel of the Lord and that he was greatly blessed to see this angel. A big smile appeared on Timmy's face.

"I believe God wants me to know he sent this angel to always take care of me 'cause my daddy can't be around anymore," he told Judith. She nodded in agreement. Their prayers for Timmy had been answered.[51]

Angels Engaged in Spiritual Warfare

Juan and Danny's parents were divorced, and the boys spent weekends with their dad. This one particular weekend, their dad's apartment was being painted, and the boys were going to stay with him at his new girlfriend's apartment.

Dad tucked them into their bed and then said, "Margarita and I are going for a walk. You all go to sleep now."

Juan felt himself drifting off to sleep but suddenly Danny poked him. "What? What," he whispered.

"Look at the ceiling! There are monsters up there. They are staring at me."

Juan looked but couldn't see anything. "You're just imagining things, Danny," he said. "Go to sleep."

A few moments passed, and Danny poked Juan again. "They're still there. They're so ugly. I'm scared."

Juan looked again and, astonished, he saw a face, then another, and another. They were hideous. They looked like pictures of devils he had seen in books. The ceiling kept changing, revealing more and more of them. Now Juan was as frightened as Danny.

The boys remembered their mom had told them that whenever they were afraid, they could ask God to send his angels to protect them. The boys began to pray, "Angels help us. Angels help us. Angels help us."

As they prayed, the ceiling began to change. First, it faded into white. Then, an angel appeared in the right corner, a large winged warrior.

"Do you see it, Danny?" Juan whispered.

"Yes, an angel!" Danny answered. "And look, there's another and another!"

Enthralled, the boys watched as big, strong angels filled the air above them—as scenes shifted one after the other. Each scene brought more angels, pushing the ugly faces to the edges of the room.

"They are fighting for us," Juan stated in awe. Slowly, the devils gave way until only the angels remained, wonderful beings who surrounded the boys and made them feel safe, cozy, and warm. They fell into a peaceful sleep.

Later, their mom did some research and eventually learned that Margarita and her friends had been using the apartment for witchcraft rituals, seances, and occult activities. Juan and Danny had seen the evil spirits that had been invited in.[52]

An Angel Appears in the Knick of Time

The summer of 1952 was magical for sixteen-year-old Bob and his two friends. They loved taking their boat out on one of the tributaries of the Ashley River near Charleston, South Carolina and waterskiing all day.

One day, they ventured off their normal course to a tidal lake, giving them more room for their fancy ski maneuvers. As they sped along the water's surface, Bob, on the skis, couldn't see another boat on the lake and relished their complete privacy.

Suddenly, without warning, the boat sputtered, and Bob went down in the water. His friends yelled out that they'd go get it fixed and be back as soon as possible. Bob, a very poor swimmer, had dropped the rope and was quite a distance from the shore. He also wasn't wearing a life preserver. The boat had rounded the corner and gotten out of earshot, so Bob was on his own.

After about ten minutes, the boat had not returned, and Bob, treading water but already tired from a long day of skiing, was beginning to panic. Frantically, he began praying, asking God for help.

Just when he thought he couldn't stay up another minute, a rickety old boat pulled up behind him manned by an elderly gentleman wearing a hat. "Do you need help?" he asked.

Bob, almost too tired to speak, managed to nod "Yes."

The man helped Bob into the boat and headed toward the only dock on the lake. He didn't say a word. When they arrived at the dock, Bob got out and collapsed from exhaustion. When he turned around to thank the man, the boat was nowhere in sight.

"You would think anyone kind enough to pull me out of the water and get me to a dock would ask, 'Is there anything else I can do for you? Do you need anything?'" said Bob.

Only an angel would have known Bob's friends would return shortly and take care of him.[53]

Summary

Angels have a special role to play in the care and upbringing of children. At a time when they can't protect themselves and may not even have two earthly parents to protect them, God is working through his angels to comfort, protect, deliver, and heal these little ones.

Assignments and Hierarchies

"The archangels are those who have stood the test of great responsibility… Yet they remain humble servants, never seeking their own glory, but always pointing to the glory of God."

C. S. Lewis

Is there an angel hierarchy? Are some angels more powerful than others, and do some have more authority? Yes, but the scholars disagree on how many levels. All authorities concede there is at least one archangel, Michael, a prince who leads the Lord's warriors. Michael is also identified as the guardian angel of Israel.[54] So, we know he is of a higher rank than other angels and is charged with guarding an entire nation.

Hierarchies

The Catholics subscribe to the nine-level theory. This dates back to a sixth-century monk who wrote under the pseudonym of Dionysius the Areopagite. (Dionysius was Paul's first convert in Athens.) In his book, *The Celestial Hierarchy*, he attempted to produce a nine-tiered organization of the angels based on statements made by the Apostle Paul in Ephesians and Colossians.

Ephesians 6:12: "For our struggle is not against enemies of blood and flesh, but against the rulers, against the authorities, against the cosmic powers of this present darkness, against the spiritual forces of evil in the heavenly places."

Colossians 1:16: "For in him all things in heaven and on earth were created, things visible and invisible, whether thrones or dominions or rulers or powers—all things have been created through him and for him."

According to Dionysius, the nine orders of angels were seraphim, cherubim, thrones, dominions, virtues, powers, principalities, archangels, and angels. The angels did not differ in moral perfection—only in their function in God's divine economy.

The first three levels, according to Dionysius, worship and adore God. The seraphim worship God for who he is; the cherubim worship God for what he has created, and the thrones worship God for his power and divine judgments.

The next three levels fulfill God's providential plans for the universe. The dominions command the lesser angels below them. The virtues receive their commands from the dominions and run the universe, especially the heavenly bodies. The powers serve the virtues by fighting evil spirits that try to stop them from fulfilling God's plan.

The principalities care for cities, states, and nations, protecting them from evil. The archangels carry God's important messages to mankind. The ordinary angels are the guardian angels, guarding humans—one guardian angel for each human.[55]

Centuries later, the great theologian Thomas Aquinas adopted Dionysius' theory of the angel hierarchy and repeated it in his famous multi-volume treatise, *Summa Theologica*. Aquinas was so interested in angels and wrote so much about them that he was called the Angelic Doctor.

Many Catholic writers on the subject of angels subscribe to the nine-level theory stemming from Dionysius. However, Mortimer Adler points out in his book, *The Angels and Us*, that modern theologians, both Catholic and Protestant, no longer regard Dionysius' nine levels as an authoritative source of theological doctrine concerning angels.[56]

The Protestants and Angel Hierarchies

The Protestant reformers wanted to back up everything with the Word of God. The Bible does not say there are nine levels of angels, although it does mention some of the terms used by Dionysius found in Paul's letters to the Ephesians and Colossians. Using these, Dionysius imagined a divine chain of command. The Reformers, however, refused to accept the theory and have come to their own conclusions, which, generally speaking, range from two levels of angels to an infinite number of angels (with each angel being its own level).

The Protestant Bible mentions three angels by name: Michael, Gabriel, and Lucifer (who rebelled against God and was thrown out of heaven). The Apocrypha, part of the Catholic Canon, adds a fourth—Raphael. Sacred Jewish writings mention yet a fifth—Uriel.

Some Protestant scholars conclude that the angels Michael, Gabriel, and Raphael (even though he is only mentioned in the Apocrypha) are archangels and are given assignments by God. He would not assign to less powerful angels.

The only angel given the title archangel in the Bible, however, is Michael.[57] Other Protestant leaders conclude Michael is, therefore, the only archangel.

Jewish Angel Hierarchies

The Jewish angelic hierarchy is established in the Hebrew Bible, Talmud, Rabbinic literature, and traditional Jewish liturgy. They are categorized in different hierarchies proposed by various theologians. For example, Maimonides, in his *Mishneh Torah*, counts ten ranks of angels. While Jewish scholars have different names for the ten ranks, they agree on ten levels.

Maimonides ranks chayot ha kodesh as the highest order of angels. They are known for their enlightenment and are responsible for holding up God's throne. They also hold the Earth in its proper position in space.

The next rank, the ophanim, guard God's throne. They are known for their wisdom, and they never sleep.

Next is the erelim, known for their courage and understanding, followed by the hashmallim, known for their love, kindness, and grace.

Seraphim come next and are known for their work for justice. The prophet Isaiah had a vision of the seraphim angels near God in heaven.[58] "Seraphs were in attendance above him; each had six wings; with two they covered their faces, and with two they covered their feet, and with two they flew. And one called to one another and said, 'Holy, holy, holy is the Lord of hosts; the whole earth is full of his glory.'"

Malakhim follow the seraphim and are known for their beauty and mercy. Elohim follow and are known for their commitment to the victory of good over evil. Bene elohim focus their work on giving glory to God and are led by the famous archangel, Michael, according to Maimonides.

Cherubim help people deal with sin that separates them from God as they seek to draw people closer to God. Finally, the ishim, the lowest level, is the closest to humans and focuses on building God's kingdom on earth.[59]

The Seven Angels before the Throne of God

The Apostle John, in his Revelation, tells us seven spirits stand before the throne of God.[60] These seven archangels are believed to form a privileged circle because they are the closest to Almighty God. Who are they, and what do they do?

There is a general agreement on four: Michael, Gabriel, Raphael, and Uriel. After that, scholars differ in the ones chosen to stand before God. Sources written centuries ago that did not make the cut into the Bible give us insights into who these mighty princes might be.

When the Archangel Gabriel appeared before Zacharias to tell him he would be the father of John the Baptist, and Zacharias doubted him, he told Zacharias he was one of the angels who stood before the throne of God.[61]

The Apocrypha gives us another example of self-identification in being one of the angels who stand in the presence of God. The Archangel Raphael told Tobias that he was one of the seven. "I am Raphael, one of the seven angels who stand ready and enter before the glory of the Lord."[62]

Each of the Archangels has an area of focus. Archangel Michael is the commander-in-chief of the Lord's armies. Archangel Gabriel appears to be the chief communications officer entrusted with important messages delivered to humans. Archangel Raphael is the chief medical officer and is responsible for healing and assisting those on earth in the healing professions. Archangel Uriel is in charge of repentance, salvation, and assisting artists, writers, and all creative people.

After these four, scholars differ in who rounds out the sacred seven. According to Dionysius, the Areopagite who imagined the nine levels of angels to which the Catholics subscribe, the remaining three are Chamuel (angel of divine justice), Jophile (chief intelligence officer and angel of wisdom, understanding, and judgment), and Zadkiel (angel of mercy, benevolence, and patron of those who forgive), but other ancient scholars have their own lists.

Of course, we would like for the hierarchy and the angels who stand in the presence of God to be clearly spelled out for us, like the twelve disciples are. On this side of heaven, we must accept what we have been given. As the Apostle Paul says, "For now we see in a mirror, dimly, but then we will see face to face. Now I know only in part; then I will know fully, even as I have been fully known."[63]

Angel Assignments

Are some angels assigned to guard cities, states, and nations? The only guidance from the Bible names Michael as the prince assigned to guard Israel (Daniel 12). If Israel has an angel assigned to guard it, wouldn't it stand to reason that other nations would as well?

One writer says that mystical writers confirm the legend that every temple, cathedral, abbey, and church is placed under the direction of a presiding angel. Furthermore, they say, every great civilization has a master angel who guides it according to some divine plan toward a worldwide order.[64]

What about us humans? Do we each have a guardian angel assigned to guard us? Once again, scholars differ. Some even say we each have two guardian angels assigned to us.

The main argument for the guardian angel assigned to each of us comes from Matthew 18:10, "Take care that you do not despise one of these little ones; for, I tell you, in heaven their angels continually see the face of my Father in heaven."

Advocates of the everyone-has-a-guardian-angel theory claim this verse makes clear that each child has his or her own guardian angel. Others say not necessarily so. It could just be referring to angels assigned generally to guard them.

St. Patrick of Ireland believed he had a guardian angel named Victoricus who appeared to him in dreams and visions. He wrote in one of his prayers: "I arise today in the might of the Cherubim; in obedience of angels; in ministration of archangels."[65]

Pope Pius XI once told a group of visitors that he prayed to his guardian angel every morning and every evening.[66]

Dr. Peter Kreeft, author of *Angels (and Demons)*, says he and his wife have guardian angels, and their names are Francis and Frodo. Dr. Kreeft dedicated his book to them.

John Calvin, on the other hand, doubted that the Scripture quoted in Matthew justifies the conclusion that every child has his or her own guardian angel. Calvin prefers to think that not one angel only has the care of every one of us but all the angels together, with one consent, watch over our salvation.[67]

Summary

We are left with opposing views about the angelic hierarchies without a clear answer from the Word of God. We should take comfort, however, in the Word, which promises us the protection and ministry of angels. All Christian scholars agree on that. My favorite angel scripture is Psalm 91. There are so many stories about the protective power of this Psalm that books have been written about it. The promise that God will command his angels concerning us to guard us in all our ways (Psalm 91:11) is one I pray daily over myself, my family, and my ministry partners. I see the angels hovering over us, watching for any danger and cutting it off at the onset. How many times they have saved us from danger, destruction, and death? We will only know when we get to heaven. Until then, I thank God we are not alone in dealing with the evil around us and the known and unknown dangers we encounter.

Angels Singing and Worshiping

*"What know we of the blest above but
that they sing and that they love?"*

William Wordsworth

Do angels sing? What does the Bible tell us?
Probably the clearest passage on this issue is Job 38:7, which says that at the creation of the world, "morning stars sang together and all the angels shouted for joy." In the parallelism of Hebrew poetry, the "morning stars" are equated with the "angels," and the joyful shouts parallel the singing. The Hebrew word for shouting also means singing.

The Apostle John, in his Revelation, tells us, "I heard a company of Angels around the Throne, the Animals, and the Elders—ten thousand times ten thousand their number, thousand after thousand after thousand in full song: The slain lamb is worthy! Take the power, the wealth, the wisdom, the strength! Take the honor, the glory, the blessing!"[68]

When Jesus was born, the gospel writer, Luke, describes the heavenly messengers who appeared to the shepherds in the field. "Then an angel of the Lord stood before them, and the glory of the Lord shone around them, and they were terrified. But the angel said to them, 'Do not be afraid; for see—I am bringing you good news of great joy for all the people: to you is born this day in the city of David a Savior, who is the Messiah, the Lord....' And suddenly there was with the angel a multitude of the heavenly host, praising God and saying, 'Glory to God in the highest heaven, and on earth peace among those whom he favors.'"[69]

Angels Singing Today

People experiencing near-death experiences tell us of heavenly music and the choirs of angels.

Dr. Eben Alexander, a neurosurgeon, wrote a best-selling book titled *Proof of Heaven*, in which he describes his near-death experience, claiming to have heard heavenly music beyond anything he had ever experienced on earth.

Anita Moorjani, the author of *Dying to Be Me*, shared her near-death experience in which she claims to have experienced a realm of beautiful music and a sense of interconnectedness and unconditional love.

Colton Burpo, a young boy who had a near-death experience during an emergency surgery, reported hearing angelic music and seeing choirs of angels while he was in heaven. His story is recounted in the book *Heaven is for Real*.

Dr. Mary Neal, an orthopedic surgeon who was involved in a kayaking accident in Chile and pinned under the kayak underwater, tells of her near-death experience in her book, *To Heaven and Back*. Dr. Neal explains that she heard a beautiful chorus of voices and felt a profound sense of love and peace.

Akiane Kramarik is an artist known for her prodigious talent and spiritual artwork. She claims to have had visions of heaven, including hearing celestial music, which she has translated into her paintings.

Mellen-Thomas Benedict shared his near-death experience, which he claims included hearing music that was "the original sound that creates life," and it conveyed a profound sense of love and unity.

Although near-death experiences are subjective, if enough people who have experienced them tell us the same thing, it lends credibility to their reports.

The Heavenly Choir

The heavenly choir, whether performing for those in heaven or for those on earth, must be far more magnificent than anything we have ever heard or experienced. Can you imagine the harmonies, the range of voices, and the majesty of the music? And all of it to glorify the King of Kings and Lord of Lords.

Perhaps there is no better choir on earth than The Mormon Tabernacle Choir, 360 voices under the direction of a musical genius. When we listen to their glorious music, we are transported to another realm. The harmonious fusion of sopranos, altos, tenors, and basses creates a celestial tapestry of sound that transcends mere music. Like a brushstroke on canvas, each voice contributes its unique hue, tone, and texture, producing a masterpiece of auditory artistry.

If an earthly choir can accomplish this, can we even imagine what a heavenly choir with thousands upon thousands of angelic voices sounds like?

Angels Join in Praise and Worship

Angels are drawn to meetings where people are praising and worshiping God. It is in their nature to praise God continuously, so they cannot resist joining us when we praise and worship.

Sometimes, angels are heard and not seen. Kathi Smith shares a story of a healing service her pastor had for those diagnosed with cancer and other dreaded illnesses. Kathi, herself recently diagnosed with cancer, was sitting with friends four rows from the back of her church and felt the presence of the Lord in a powerful way. As the service proceeded with special music, Kathi heard several male tenor voices behind her. She turned to see if she knew these men with remarkable voices but no one was there. Yet, she kept hearing them. Kathi turned to one of her friends sitting with her who used to sing in a choir and asked if she heard them. She smiled and said yes, but she couldn't see them either. Kathi concluded it was a heavenly chorus of angels that gave her and others great comfort and joy.[70]

Singing Angel in the ICU

A nurse recounts the story an ICU patient shared with her. She entered the patient's room to take some X-rays and felt God wanted to heal the young man there in the bed. He was on a ventilator and only semi-conscious. The nurse asked the man's girlfriend, who was with him, if she could pray for him. The girlfriend agreed enthusiastically. As the nurse was about to pray, a doctor walked in, and she had to leave without praying.

The nurse went to the patient's room when her shift ended, and the girlfriend said the doctor had seen steady improvement and was going to take her boyfriend off the ventilator the next morning. The nurse and girlfriend stood on either side of the bed and prayed for God to heal the young man. He nodded in agreement.

The two women exchanged phone numbers, and the girlfriend sent a text message to the nurse after she left, inviting her to come back and visit and pray again.

A week later, the nurse was finally free to do a follow-up visit to this young man. He had been moved out of the ICU and was off the ventilator. As the nurse approached the bed, the man told her a remarkable story. The night she and his girlfriend prayed, he saw not two but three people around his bed. The nurse was at his right, his girlfriend was at the left, and at the foot of the bed, there was a woman singing gospel songs. He told the nurse he had never had an experience like that before and believed the woman was an angel sent to minister God's love to him.[71]

There's a Song in the Air

The Welsh Revival of 1859 was a Christian religious revival that swept through Wales during the nineteenth century and was characterized by a significant outpouring of religious fervor and spiritual awakening, leading to a renewed interest in Christianity and the conversion of many individuals to the faith.

One of the remarkable aspects of the Welsh Revival was the occurrence of spontaneous and often unexplained phenomena, including "singing in the air" or "singing in the heavens." According to various accounts from that time, people reported hearing angelic or heavenly music during revival meetings, even when there was no visible source for the music.

Witnesses claimed that this ethereal music was extraordinarily beautiful and often indescribable in its splendor. The music was said to be so enchanting that it had a profound and transformative effect on those who experienced it, rendering them incapable of movement while they were listening. It was considered a manifestation of the Holy Spirit's presence and a sign of God's approval of the revival.

The Welsh Revival was marked by a sense of awe, deep repentance, and spiritual renewal among the people. This "singing in the air" phenomenon was just one of the many extraordinary occurrences reported during the revival, including mass conversions, fervent prayer, and transformed lives.[72]

Angels Singing in the Grotto

In 1858, Bernadette Soubirous, a young girl from Lourdes, reported apparitions of the Virgin Mary. One day, while out gathering firewood with her sister and a friend, she had a vision of the Virgin and heard angelic voices singing hymns she had never heard before. She described the music as soothing and gentle. The Virgin appeared to her on eighteen occasions, instructing her to build a church at the grotto site where she experienced the apparitions.

After extensive interrogation, the Catholic Church determined her visions were genuine. Bernadette was canonized in 1933 by Pope Pius XI. The town of Lourdes has become a major international pilgrimage site, attracting millions of visitors each year. Several churches and infrastructures were built around the cave where the apparitions occurred, forming together the Sanctuary of Our Lady of Lourdes. The sanctuary is known for the Lourdes water streaming inside the cave from a spring discovered by Bernadette during the apparitions, which is said to have healing properties, attracting sick pilgrims.

Angels Joining in Worship

Elias Arguello and his wife, Diana, are praise and worship leaders in Argentina. When they were only twenty-one and twenty years old, they decided to worship God by singing and recording music for many hours each day. Early on, they realized that they were hearing other voices joining them. They believe those voices are angels singing with them. They have recorded over ninety hours of music that includes the sounds of angels and other sounds that they believe are from heaven.

An unexplained phenomenon of their process is that the angels do not join the singing when only one of them is in the recording booth. The angels will accompany the music if both of the pair are in the studio, even if just one of them sings.

You can listen to a recording with the angels joining the Arguellos at the website www.comequicklyministries.org/blog/worshipping-angels/

Summary

Angels praise and worship God the Father, Son, and Holy Spirit in heaven. Those who have heard their music through near-death experiences or otherwise tell us of its soothing and healing power. When we enter into true praise and worship on earth, the angels are drawn to it and join us. We may not see them, but angels cannot stay away where there is a body of believers worshiping and praising God.

10

The Comforting Angels

"Angels are heralds of eternity sent to help mankind break through when they cannot break out."

Graham Cooke

We serve a tender-hearted God who is full of compassion, bringing comfort in all of our troubles. God cares about our feelings. When we hurt, he hurts with us.

Isaiah brought hope to an exiled nation when he wrote, "Comfort, O comfort my people, says your God." And, "The Lord has comforted his people, and will have compassion on his suffering ones." And, "As a mother comforts her child, so will I comfort you."[73]

While God depends on his sons and daughters to bring comfort to those who are sick, imprisoned, in need of food, clothing, and shelter, and emotionally distraught, he also sends his angels when needed.

Comfort in a Medically Fragile Situation

Virginia and Jim rushed to the Ashville, North Carolina, hospital near the ski slopes where their teenage son, Thomas, had suffered a terrible accident. They thought maybe he had a concussion and were anxious to get him home and into the care of his regular physician.

They arrived to find a doctor waiting for them. He carefully explained that Thomas' injuries, traumatic to his brain, were far beyond their capabilities to handle. As such phrases as "permanent brain damage" and "a life-threatening situation" were spoken, Virginia cried in despair. Thomas was in a coma, unable to communicate.

The doctor recommended that Thomas be transferred to a level-one trauma center in Atlanta, Georgia, to give him the best chance of survival and recovery. While waiting for the ambulance to arrive, Virginia was thankful for the young nurse who told her, "He's young. There's hope." It was the only positive thing she had heard.

As Thomas arrived at Grady Memorial Hospital in Atlanta and was taken to the Marcus Stroke and Neuroscience Center, Virginia collapsed on the floor of his room in tears at the thought of losing her boy. As she cried in desperation, a nurse walked in and introduced herself as April. She sat down on the floor with Virginia and was positive, encouraging, and kind as she told Virginia and Jim about another patient who had been in a motorcycle accident. She outlined his traumatic injury, his treatment, and his recovery—telling them he now had a job and a girlfriend and was healing well. She said he had been in the bed where Thomas was now lying. Her calm words reassured Virginia, and she was able to get a little sleep.

The next day Virginia and Jim met the director of the center and shared with him their wonderful experience with April. He said he'd hand-picked all of the nurses in the center and didn't know anyone named April. When the day nurse,

Lulu, came in, and Virginia told her about April, she said, "We don't have any nurses here named April." Virginia continued to ask, describing April in detail, but no one had ever heard of or seen a nurse named April fitting the description Virginia gave. They told her no visiting nurses had been there either. Virginia said she knew then that April at Grady was an angel sent to her and Jim to bring comfort to their troubled hearts.

After several days in a coma, Thomas woke up. During those days, Virginia's church had a prayer vigil for him. As he began talking, doctors were amazed, calling his recovery a "miracle."[74]

Touched by an Angel

Paul Swope ran home from school with his report card, looking forward to his mom praising the good grades he had received. When he bounced through the door of his house, he knew something was wrong. His sister Hazel, age sixteen, had a frightened look on her face, and his baby sister was crying in her playpen. He wondered why his grandmother was there.

Paul ran into his mom's bedroom and saw a doctor leaning over his mom with a stethoscope. His dad sat in a corner, running his hands through his hair. The doctor stood up and shook his head. Hazel started screaming.

Paul's grandmother took his hand and led him gently from the room for a talk. His mother had been weak for several days and had finally succumbed to her illness.

Paul couldn't believe it until they took his mother's body away. He prayed his mom would come back to him because he was so close to her. She had rocked his baby sister every night and read to Paul, who sat at her feet as she rocked. Paul sat in her rocking chair, trying to remember all the songs and stories she had sung and told. As his baby sister got older, she would put her hand in Paul's hair and playfully pull. Paul's mom did not miss a beat as she loosened the baby's grip and tenderly stroked her son's hair back in place.

Imagining the happy times didn't help. After the funeral, Paul would lay in his bed sobbing night after night. He was so alone. Dad was almost never home. Grandma moved in but spent most of her time caring for the baby.

Paul begged and prayed for his mom to come back. Then, one night, as he cried in bed, he felt a cool hand stroking his forehead and straightening his hair as if his baby sister had tugged it again. It was *Mother!* He reached out to grab the hand from heaven and not let it go. The warm, soft fingers spoke of a powerful love that penetrated him deeply. Peace flowed over him.

Although the pain of loss continued after that night, Paul now knew he was not alone. He felt his mom was watching over him and continued to feel it through his childhood, adolescence, while in a battlefield hell in France during World War II, to the raising of a family of his own.

Even when he was dying, his widow, Alice, said Paul knew his mom could see him and cared for him. Paul Swope, known for his kindness, died at age seventy-four.[75]

Are Angels in Disguise?

I have a theory that almost everyone has had an angel experience, but most of us don't know it. Angels can incarnate as humans and not be detected. How, then, would we know an angel had visited us or come to our assistance? In some cases, the angel appearing human disappears immediately after rendering aid. Several testimonies in this book fall into that category. The person the angel helped turns to thank the angel and no one is there.

Martin Niemöller was a pastor in Germany during Hitler's oppressive reign in World War II. Niemöller refused to yield to Hitler's demands. His church was bombed, and he was imprisoned. As his trial began in February of 1938, a guard led him from his prison cell to an imposing courtroom. Niemöller became frightened for his church and family because he knew they were in danger. And unknown terrors awaited him as well. As he ascended the stairs into the courtroom, he heard a whisper. His guard was quoting Proverbs 18:10 to him. "The name of the Lord is a strong tower; the righteous run into it and are safe."

This word from God sustained him through his trial and the dreary years of imprisonment in Nazi concentration camps until he could minister again.[76]

What are the chances that one of Hitler's guards would be quoting Scripture to a prisoner who pushed back against Hitler? Might that guard have been an angel sent to encourage a frightened and discouraged pastor? I think he easily could have been.

Angel Comforting Woman in a Wreck

Angel (her real name) was driving from Fredericksburg, Virginia, to Greenville, South Carolina, one early Sunday morning. She was on a back two-lane road when she fell asleep at the wheel. As she lost control of the car, it turned around several times before crashing into a tree.

Miraculously, Angel was not hurt, just stunned and numbed by the experience. Her car was totaled. As she contemplated what to do, a lady, nicely dressed, drove up and stopped beside her on the road. The lady suggested she call a relative, so Angel called her grandparents back in Fredericksburg, who immediately agreed to come to where she was to help. It was about a two-hour drive.

Angel said she was more or less "out of it" but was so glad to have the company of such a nice lady who promised to stay until her grandparents arrived. Angel can't remember what they talked about—just that she was there and kept assuring Angel she wouldn't leave her.

The grandparents finally arrived, and Angel fell into their arms, sobbing, knowing they would take over and help her get home. As Angel turned to thank the nice lady who had stayed with her and calmed her, she was nowhere to be seen. Angel then knew a heavenly visitor had provided comfort for her in her time of need.[77]

Angel Comfort in the Loss of a Child

Marilynn married young, and her husband turned out to be an alcoholic. She soon found herself pregnant and, after five and a half months, gave birth to a preemie weighing two and a half pounds. Marilynn named her Colette, and she was the one bright spot in Marilynn's life.

Colette came home from the hospital and had gotten up to seven pounds when she suddenly died of crib death. Marilynn was devastated. Having no one to turn to, she began hammering God with questions: Why did this happen? How could you let an innocent child die? Is she suffering?

Marilynn couldn't cope. She knew she needed help and felt like she was dying. She asked God to help her not be afraid. Night after night, she prayed and noticed that a comforting feeling would come over her.

"God, is that you?" she asked. She opened her eyes, and an angel appeared. The angel changed her thoughts. With the angel, she realized that Colette had been a gift from God, even for the short time she was with Marilynn. God loved baby Colette and would care for her in heaven.

Marilynn believed God sent an angel to her because there was no one else to express his love for her. The angel helped her see that God doesn't cause suffering but suffers along with us.[78]

Angel Providing Strength to a Mother

Nita knew her daughter was dying. She prayed God would take her first so she would not have to endure such a great loss, thinking she would lose her mind if her daughter died at a young age. It was not to be.

Nita could not go to the funeral. She arranged for a private viewing of her daughter at the funeral home. She went into the chapel and just stood there. As she saw her daughter in the casket from afar, she couldn't move.

"Lord Jesus," she prayed. "Please go with me, or I will not be able to go to her." Instantly, a strong presence came to her side, so powerful she could feel it. The presence took her arm, and a voice said, "Come. I'll go with you." Nita looked to see who was there but saw no one. She only felt the presence.

Nita started walking. Where she had been feeble, she could now walk boldly to the casket. She felt strong and well and could gaze at her beautiful daughter's face. Nita sat by her daughter's side, and while she was sad, she was not devastated, hysterical, or overcome. The presence stood beside her the whole time. Nita thought of the angel sent to comfort Christ in the Garden of Gethsemane and knew that God had sent an angel to comfort and strengthen her in her moment of need. She kissed her daughter's cold face, held her cold hands, and whispered as she turned to leave, "I'll see you in our Father's house."[79]

Comfort to Children in the Night

Norah Norris was six years old, living at a boarding school run by her four spinster aunts. These were good ladies, but they were very strict on discipline, so when young Norah awoke one night after a nightmare, she knew not to run to them. Instead, she quietly cried until she could go to sleep again. The nightmares occurred more and more frequently. One night, she dreamed that a fierce black and orange dog was attacking her. When she awoke, she found the apparent likeness of the dog silhouetted in the moonlight on the wall behind her bed. Little Norah was terrified. She closed her eyes and prayed a little prayer that she had been taught, "Lord, keep me safe this night, secure from all my fears. May angels guard me while I sleep 'til morning light appears."

As Norah opened her eyes, she saw a figure beside her. Norah described the figure as having feathered wings and a beautiful head. It stayed for just a moment and then left her, but she knew she had seen an angel who was there to keep her safe. As Norah looked up, the dog shadow had vanished, and Norah had a lovely, peaceful feeling and was no longer afraid.

In the morning, she told her aunts, and they were extremely kind to her as they listened and questioned her about her nightly visitor. The memory of seeing the angel never left Norah, and she never doubted that it was really an angel sent to comfort her in her terror.

Norah says it has been a joy throughout her life that a special messenger was sent to her to quiet the trembling fears of God's terrified child. She has told this story to many other children she has taught through the years.

Mary was evacuated to a small village in Britain during World War II. She was seven years old and sent to live in a rambling old house that seemed to her to be enormous. Mary was always frightened in the dark, and while in bed, she held on tightly to the sheets. One night, she woke feeling something gently stroking her head, so she pulled back the sheet to see what it was. There beside her was a figure in white kneeling. As Mary watched, the figure did not move, but Mary felt a bit frightened and started to run out of the room. When she looked back, the figure had gone, and Mary soon realized it was an angel. She was never again afraid of the dark.

Chris was camping with his schoolmates, where they were to set up a place for a summer school camp. The wind was strong but they did get a tent set up the first day. During the stormy night it started raining with lightning and thunder. Chris and his friend, Matthew, woke up and saw a bright light surrounding their tent. Opening the flap, they were startled to see angels. Chris said they were very tall and dressed in white. The light emanated from the angels, and one of the boys thought of the verse from Joshua, "Be strong and very courageous." The boys took great comfort from their heavenly bodyguard and slept peacefully despite the threatening weather.[80]

Summary

When we are emotionally sick or distraught, we need a divine comforter. Our comforter has many assistants, most of them ordinary human beings. Haven't we all comforted someone at his or her point of need? Haven't we been comforted by friends, family, and professionals when we need help?

If there is no human God can use, he will send an angel. When someone in need doesn't know how to ask for help, God will send an angel. God will not leave us comfortless. The Good Shepherd takes care of his sheep.

11

Heaven's Warriors

"For he will command his angels concerning you to guard you in all your ways."

Psalm 91:11

Angels have many roles. We usually think of them as providing comforting, rescuing services, but they are fierce, powerful beings who are sometimes called upon to attack armies fighting counter to God's will or protect those in harm's way. When unsavory people target God's children, angels appear in whatever form is appropriate to protect them from harm. When they engage in battle, no human foe can stand against them. The most dramatic example I can think of from the Bible is the angel who fought for King Hezekiah.

Angel of Deliverance

King Hezekiah of Judah faced a terrifying military threat from the king of Assyria, King Sennacherib. Sennacherib sent messengers to Hezekiah, asking him to surrender before any battle took place. The messengers pointed out that no army assembled against their king had defeated him and promised the same fate for the Judeans. Even the God of Israel could not deliver them and taunted the messengers.

When Hezekiah heard this, he tore his clothes, went into the house of the Lord, and called for the prophet, Isaiah, to pray. Isaiah sent word back to the king to fear not. He said God would put a spirit in the king of Assyria. He would hear a rumor, causing him to return to his land where the sword would kill him.

Once again, the messengers appeared and threatened to destroy Hezekiah and his people. This time, Hezekiah took their threatening letter and went into the temple, spreading it before the Lord God. He prayed a passionate prayer:

"And Hezekiah prayed to the Lord, saying: 'O Lord of hosts, God of Israel, who are enthroned above the cherubim, you are God, you alone, of all the kingdoms of the earth; you have made heaven and earth. Incline your ear, O Lord, and hear; open your eyes, O Lord, and see; hear all the words of Sennacherib, which he has sent to mock the living God. Truly, O Lord, the kings of Assyria have laid waste all the nations and their lands, and have hurled their gods into the fire, though they were no gods, but the work of human hands—wood and stone—and so they were destroyed. So now, O Lord our God, save us from his hand, so that all the kingdoms of the earth may know that you alone are the Lord.'"[81]

Isaiah returned and told King Hezekiah that because he had prayed to God concerning the situation with King Sennacherib, he would not come into Jerusalem, shoot an arrow in it, come before it with a shield, or cast up a siege ramp against it. "For I will defend this city to save it, for my own sake and for the sake of my servant, David."[82]

Then the angel of the Lord set out and, in one night, struck down 185,000 soldiers in the camp of the Assyrians. When morning dawned, they were all dead. King Sennacherib left and went home. As Isaiah had prophesied, when Sennacherib was worshiping in the temple of his god, Nisroch, his sons came in with a sword and assassinated him.

In this incredible story, one angel killed 185,000 soldiers in one night without engaging in battle. Perhaps this was germ warfare at its finest, but however the angel managed this feat, it was not something any of the humans in the story could have done.

Sometimes, we think remarkable things that happened thousands of years ago are not still happening today, but stories from World Wars I and II, the Yom Kippur War, and the Gulf War between Israel and Syria prove otherwise.

Angels of Mons during World War I

August of 1914 found the German armies overpowering those of France, Belgium, and Britain, sweeping aside all resistance. The fighting was intense, and the Allied soldiers were exhausted from lack of sleep and inadequate provisions. The British Expeditionary Force (BEF), in particular, was on the verge of collapse. When word reached Great Britain that they were outnumbered three to one and facing imminent defeat, the entire nation of Britain responded with prayer. Saints filled the churches, calling out to God for deliverance.

On August 26, the forces clashed at Mons, a city in Belgium. At one critical point in the battle, the BEF was retreating with the German cavalry in hot pursuit. Suddenly, the German artillery barrage fell silent. The British soldiers reported four or five white-robed beings, much larger than people, hovering between them and the Germans. They faced the German army, holding out their hands as if to say, "Halt!" The Germans began a hasty retreat. Despite the overwhelming odds, the Allied forces had time to regroup and establish a solid defensive position.

Several British soldiers reported seeing the angels. One officer said a squadron of phantom cavalry escorted his battalion for twenty minutes. Other soldiers in a small British battalion, about to be overrun by German infantrymen, said they became aware of a shadowy army fighting beside them. These other-worldly warriors fought with bows and arrows, wearing the armor worn centuries before. German prisoners of war said they were surprised to see their British opponents reverting to wearing armor and shooting arrows. The fact so many of the soldiers reported the sightings lent authenticity to the intervention of angels in the Battle of Mons.[83]

The Angel Protecting the Finnish Army

In the winter of 1939, three months after the outbreak of World War II, Russia invaded Finland. On Christmas Eve, at Taipan, on the Karelian Isthmus, the Finnish army was exhausted and almost out of supplies and ammunition. Suddenly, a brilliant light brought the fighting to a halt. As the soldiers' eyes adjusted, they saw a shining angel holding a luminous cross pointed toward Finland. The hostilities ceased for the evening, and the bone-tired soldiers slept after three days of round-the-clock fighting. Supplies were brought in that turned the tide of the battle.[84]

Angels Flying Planes for the British Air Force

In the early days of World War II, Britain's Air Force saved it from invasion and defeat. Some months after the war, a ceremony honored Air Force Chief Marshal Lord Hugh Dowding. The king, the prime minister, and many other dignitaries attended. The chief marshal shared a story about his legendary conflict where his pilots rarely slept and never stopped flying. Even when their planes were hit, either incapacitating pilots or killing them, the planes kept flying. Pilots in other planes would see figures still operating the controls. The chief marshal believed angels had flown the planes of those pilots who could no longer fly themselves.[85]

The Yom Kippur War

In 1973, when Israel fasted and prayed on its most holy day of the year, Yom Kippur, one hundred thousand Egyptians invaded Israel from the south, and fourteen hundred Syrian tanks invaded Israel from the north. Israel was nearly defenseless, with most of its military personnel either at home or in synagogues. In yet another version of the David and Goliath story, Israel managed to emerge victorious in the face of seemingly insurmountable odds.

During the Yom Kippur War, a small number of Israeli soldiers held back a much larger contingent of Syrian soldiers for four days in the Golan Heights. The Syrians had three infantry divisions and over a thousand tanks. At one point, Israel only had three tanks. The Israeli forces were on the verge of collapse when the Syrians retreated. A Syrian soldier later said he saw an army of angels surrounding the Israeli tanks, which is why they withdrew.

At another point, an Israeli commander, David Yinni, was in the process of pulling his troops out of a confrontation with the Syrian army when he saw they were trapped in a minefield. The troops began crawling on their bellies, using their bayonets to try and find the mines. One of the soldiers offered a heartfelt prayer. A strong wind began to blow as the soldiers hunkered down, waiting for it to pass. When it was over—much to their relief—they saw it had blown away so much of the dirt that the mines were exposed. The entire platoon escaped unharmed. Hebrews 1:7 says, "Of the angels he says, 'He makes his angels winds, and his servants flames of fire.'"[86]

Angels Fighting as Winds

In other combat zones, angels have appeared as strong winds to protect soldiers and civilians. In August 2014, a Hamas missile was in the air and aimed at Israel's Kirya (the equivalent of the US Pentagon). It could have also hit a Tel Aviv railroad station. Iron Dome, the Israeli defense system, which usually takes down missiles, was malfunctioning. It could not bring down this missile. About four seconds before the missile hit, a strong east wind came from nowhere and blew the missile into the sea. Observers were amazed and called it the hand of God that saved hundreds of lives.[87]

Another example of winds protecting soldiers comes from the Gulf War. Fifteen minutes before the ground attack on February 24, 1991, the wind reversed direction and blew in favor of the Coalition forces (even though it always blows in the other direction in that part of the world). This neutralized the threat of poison gas because the wind would have blown it right back onto the Iraqis. Four days later, cease-fire orders were issued, and the wind resumed its normal course. The commanding general, US General Krulak, attributed this miracle to prayer.[88]

Psychological Warfare

Sometimes, warrior angels simply show up and present a threat to avoid any fighting from occurring. They may, in fact, only be visible to the attackers, not to those needing protection.

Billy Graham tells the story of a Chinese missionary, Miss Monsen, suffering from malaria when her mission compound, which protected hundreds of women and children refugees, was surrounded by bandits one night. As she lay in the bed recovering, Satan harassed her: "What will you do when the looters come? When the shooting starts, are you sure those promises you have been relying on will protect you?"

Miss Monsen turned to the Lord, "Lord, I have been teaching these people all these years that your promises are true, and if they fail now, my mouth will be forever closed, and I must go home."

Miss Monsen ministered through the night despite her illness, encouraging her charges to pray and trust God to deliver them. Although it was a frightening experience, the compound made it through the night untouched. In the morning, people from the nearby neighborhoods asked Miss Monsen, "Who were those four people guarding your house last night?" She told them no one had been there, but they said, "We saw them with our own eyes!"

Miss Monsen then told them that God had sent his angels to protect his children in their hour of need.[89]

God's Perfect Bodyguards

God protects his children and seems to have just the right bodyguard for each person in danger.

Barbara, pregnant with her first child, was traveling home to Dothan, Alabama, from Winter Haven, Florida. She was scheduled to change buses in Tallahassee, Florida, and catch the bus to Dothan, which would get her home around midnight when her mom planned to meet her. Unfortunately, she missed her connection in Tallahassee and had to take a later bus, which would not get her home until the wee hours of the morning. Her mom sent her a message to wait until the next day to travel, but Barbara did not receive it.

As she sat at the station waiting for the next bus, a lady sat beside her. When Barbara asked where she was going, she replied, "Dothan, Alabama."

When they boarded the bus, the woman again sat down beside Barbara. Although they didn't talk much during the trip, Barbara felt safe with the woman. Upon arrival in Dothan, they were the only people in the dark bus station. Barbara thought it was odd that no one was there to meet her new companion, but she didn't dwell on it because she was more concerned about how she would get home herself.

One car was left in the parking lot, with a man inside. He came up to Barbara and asked if she needed a ride home. She climbed in the front seat and was surprised when the woman from the bus slid in beside her.

On the way home, the man reached over and put his hand on Barbara's leg. She jerked away and did not speak to him for the remainder of the trip. Arriving home, Barbara and the woman jumped out of the car as quickly as possible and watched the car speed off. Barbara turned to thank the woman for remaining with her, but no one was there. Barbara's mom, who had been praying for her daughter's safe return, gave thanks and praise to God for sending special protection to escort Barbara in the face of danger.[90]

In another story, a teenager had been working late and caught the bus home from her job in the dark. A man seated near her on the bus kept looking at her, making her feel quite uncomfortable. She looked away, hoping he would find something else to focus on.

When she arrived at her stop, she thought she would finally be rid of him. To her dismay, he got right off the bus with her. As soon as she stepped off the bus, she noticed a large white dog that she had never seen before moving beside her. The dog stayed by her side the entire way home. When she started up the front steps to her house, she saw that the man had disappeared.

Opening the front door to her home, she turned to give the dog a pat and a "good boy." The dog was gone, and she never saw it again.[91]

Angel Warriors in the Spiritual Realm

Of course, we have battles to fight here on earth. We need protection from those who would want to harm us. We may have to fight to stop evil. We are blessed when angels come to our aid in such times, but my guess is that nothing that we see here compares to the battles that go on in the heavenly realm between the angels of glory and the fallen angels.

Before the devil was ousted from heaven, the Bible tells us war broke out between Michael and his angels and "the dragon." The dragon (the one called the devil and Satan) and his angels fought back but were no match for Michael. After the battle, they were kicked out of heaven and thrown down to earth.[92]

Another description of heavenly warfare comes from the book of Daniel, chapters 9 and 10. Daniel, a prophet in exile, had prayed and fasted for his people, asking God for mercy. The angel, Gabriel, was dispatched to bring a message to him as soon as he began his prayer. When Gabriel arrived, he told Daniel that he would have been there twenty-one days sooner, but the prince of the Kingdom of Persia opposed him. Michael, the great archangel, came to his aid and kept the prince of the Kingdom of Persia at bay, allowing Gabriel to continue his mission and deliver the message.

I recently heard a prayer testimony from a young mom with little children left alone when her husband had to go out of town on business. They did not live in the best part of town and had no security system. One night, while he was gone, this mom felt compelled to pray 2 Kings 6:11–23 over her family. She prayed for the same protection God had given to the prophet Elisha, who had angel armies protecting him and his servant. The next morning on the news, she learned that the night before, armed robbers had used crowbars to break into apartments protected by metal bars just across the street from her. Why, she asked, didn't they target our house with no metal bars and no security system? Although she didn't see them, she and her family had the same protection as Elisha—angel armies.[93]

In his book, *Angel Armies on Assignment*, Pastor Tim Sheets says he believes we are moving into an era where angel armies, activated by the Holy Spirit, will bring to pass the decrees of the saints, helping to bring God's Kingdom to come on earth. Pastor Sheets believes our words are missiles and bombs aimed at God's enemies, and the angels will deliver our word weapons (even as airplanes deliver military bombs).

"Verbal missiles launched under Holy Spirit command will hit their mark. Verbal prophetic missiles, targeting Holy Spirit planned attacks in the spirit realm, targeting demonic princes, targeting the powers, targeting the rulers of darkness, targeting spiritual wickedness in high places…will go off.…When the [church] becomes the King's mouthpiece on earth, declaring what he says, forbidding what he says should be forbidden, and permitting what he wants to be permitted, we are going to see the chariots of fire and mighty warriors of heaven come to our aid and defense."[94]

Summary

The warrior angels are no match for humans. However they might appear—as winds, animals, shining beings, ancient warriors, or ordinary human beings—they are fierce superpowers. Not even Batman, Superman, Spider-Man, or Captain America could stand against them. Our job as saints is to learn to work with them.

In the stories we have seen, they are activated by prayer, faith, and our words declaring God's will and purposes. Pastor Sheets says we cannot think that angels only assist and appear occasionally or for some saints but not others. All of God's people have a role to play in bringing his kingdom to come on earth. In the process, we are supposed to be assisted and guarded by angels and connected to resources by them. Angels are supposed to fight with us and ensure our victories. As Pastor Sheets says, "It's time to raise the bar and stop living lowered, watered-down Christianity and begin living in Biblical reality."[95]

12

The Devil's Angels

"He said to them, 'I watched Satan fall from heaven like a flash of lightning.'"

Luke 10:18

Before God created the world, he created angels. Lucifer was perhaps the highest-ranking of all of the angels. He was beautiful, gifted, brilliant, and serving God, his creator.

At some point before the creation of mankind, Lucifer, no longer content to be God's minister, decided he wanted to be God. Persuading one-third of the heavenly host to join him, he attempted to invade and overthrow the God of the universe.

Because of his pride, Lucifer underestimated God and overestimated his own abilities. Instead of overthrowing God, Lucifer and all with him were cast down and removed from God's presence and glory. His eternal fate was set, but he and his cohorts were determined to bring as many humans down with them as they could.

Lucifer, now referred to as Satan (from the Greek meaning to oppose or act as an adversary), along with his fallen angels and demons, devised strategies to keep humans from worshiping God, receiving Jesus Christ as their Savior and Lord, and fulfilling the destinies God has ordained for them. Their strategies are aimed at keeping existing Christians on the sidelines through fear, temptations of the flesh, lust, pride, and lies and to keep those who aren't Christians from becoming followers of God's son.

For those of us who are Christians, our two biggest mistakes when it comes to Satan are to ignore him and to overestimate him. When we ignore him, we allow him and his demons to kill, steal, and destroy without opposition. When we overestimate him, we allow ourselves to be intimidated, possibly to the point of surrendering, thinking there is nothing we can do about a situation he has orchestrated.

Although I started to omit this chapter on the evil angels because I wanted this book to be about the holy angels God has given us to help us as we journey through this life on planet Earth, I decided a book about angels would not be complete if it did not include a chapter on one-third of the angels who decided to wage war against God and his children. Knowledge is power, and knowledge of how Satan and his company operate and what we can do about it is essential if we are to live the victorious lives God wants us to live. Satanic pressure is designed to make us quit. We will feel the full frontal attack in our minds, bodies, and emotions. In this chapter, I will outline the major strategies of Satan and his evil angels and highlight the weapons God has given us to combat them and defeat our enemy.

Strategies of the Enemy: Using the Desires of the Flesh

In C.S. Lewis' beloved book, *The Screwtape Letters*, a fictional account of a senior devil coaching a junior devil on accomplishing the goal of keeping the junior devil's subject from becoming a Christian, the junior devil is embarrassed to have to tell his mentor that his subject has accepted Jesus Christ as his Lord and Savior.

Going to Plan B, the senior devil says, "Well, whatever you do, keep him off his knees."

"How do I do that?" asks the junior devil.

"Easy," says the senior devil. "Every time he thinks about praying, just remind him that he is hungry."

From this one incident in Lewis' book, we get a glimpse into how the devil uses our human weaknesses to keep us from advancing as Christians.

Lies, Lies, and More Lies

Although we probably cannot know all of Satan's strategies, we can know some of his favorites. Most of his work is done in and through our minds. He sends his demons to lie to us in ways that are so subtle we think it's our own thoughts. In this way, he seeks to gain a controlling influence on his target's life. Demons get as much information as they can by observing us and then feeding us lies if we let them.

Some first-generation college graduates have had to overcome lies that they did not have the brains or the financial resources to attend college. Some children of parents with diseases such as Parkinson's or Alzheimer's have to fight lies that they, too, are bound to suffer the same illnesses. Satan will exploit every situation he can with lies made to look like truth.

He makes God's children question his love, care, and forgiveness. He lies to unbelievers, telling them that accepting Christ will result in a restrictive lifestyle stifling all creativity and enjoyment. He lies anywhere and everywhere he can.

We will see how we can cast down these lies he is feeding us with the truth of God's Word, our sword.

Fear, Worry, and Anxiety

"For God did not give us a spirit of cowardice, but rather a spirit of power and of love and of self-discipline."[96]

If God does not give us a spirit of fear, then we know it comes from Satan. Fear causes us to take our eyes off God and focus on our problem or situation. As long as the disciple, Peter, kept his eyes on Jesus, he could walk on water, but as soon as he took his eyes off his Lord and looked down at the raging sea, he became fearful and started to sink.[97]

Worry and anxiety are offshoots of fear. These negative emotions planted and sustained in our minds by the enemy keep us sidelined, unwilling to take risks for God. They weigh us down as we fail to see God as bigger than any problem we might have or unable to resolve a situation we have asked him to handle. They undermine our faith.

Satan knows if we keep our eyes on God, he is doomed. He cannot get us off course to fail. His demons bombard us with negative thoughts and attempt to cause us to look at the problem or circumstance as insurmountable.

In Mark's gospel, a father brings his son, tormented by a demon, to Jesus and says, "…But if you can do anything, have pity on us and help us."

Jesus responded, "All things can be done for the one who believes." Jesus then commanded the demon to come out of the boy, and after convulsing him on the ground, it left him. When the disciples asked Jesus why they couldn't cast out the demon, Jesus told them it was because of their lack of faith.[98] Faith in God, keeping our eyes on him, and knowing he can do all things overcomes any adverse circumstance and emotion.

Doubt

Satan loves to convince us that God's Word and his promises are not true. I recently talked to a young man who had accepted Christ as his Lord and Savior but was convinced his sins were so great that God had not forgiven him, although he had asked many times. The Bible clearly states, "If we confess our sins, he is faithful and just to forgive our sins and cleanse us from all unrighteousness."[99]

This young man did not realize he was being harassed and lied to by the enemy. Together, we spoke truth to the lies he was being told. When Satan tempted Jesus in the wilderness, Jesus countered every one of Satan's temptations with the truth of God's Word, saying, "It is written…"[100]

After we prayed, the young man said he felt so much better. He knew the next time Satan tried this trick what to do, and he understood we have to accept God's Word as truth on faith.

Speaking Word Curses

A word curse is any statement spoken to, by, or about us that is contrary to what God's Word says about us. Our tongues are powerful. In fact, Proverbs says, "Death and life are in the power of the tongue…,"[101]

These word curses are often spoken by the person about themselves. For example, "I never do anything right," "I'm a failure at everything," "If God really loved me, he wouldn't have let this happen,"" I hate myself," "I'm a lousy father," " I will never get out of debt," and on and on and on.

When we speak these word curses, Satan uses them to harass us and cause us to feel hopeless—trapped with no avenue of escape. Once we speak such negative things about ourselves, Satan and his demons can use them against us, reminding us of what we said and feeding us such garbage as "You'll fail if you try that," "No one likes you, so stay away," or "Your situation is hopeless."

I have started countering every word curse I hear or speak with a positive statement. If I speak it myself, I immediately speak the opposite of the word curse to cancel it. If my husband speaks it, I tell him I disagree and declare it canceled.

Counterfeiting

Satan is a master counterfeiter. He takes the truth and twists it so it has some semblance of truth but is devoid of truth at the core. He seeks to make false religions look like the real thing. One example is the New Age religion.

New Age religion is a diverse and eclectic spiritual movement. Central to New Age beliefs is a holistic approach to spirituality, emphasizing the interconnectedness of mind, body, and spirit. Followers often seek to achieve personal transformation and enlightenment through practices such as meditation, yoga, and alternative healing methods.

New Age spirituality tends to be syncretic, blending elements from Eastern philosophies, Western mysticism, and Indigenous spiritual practices. The movement embraces a belief in the existence of a universal energy or consciousness often referred to as the "Divine" or "Source." Many adherents explore astrology, numerology, and channeling. These practices are listed as things God hates in his Word.[102]

The New Age movement also places a strong emphasis on environmental consciousness, promoting the idea that humanity is in a spiritual and planetary awakening, which will result in a more inclusive and harmonious worldview. Of course, we should all do everything we can to protect and preserve our planet, and that part is in line with Christianity. However, the New Age movement fails to admit we humans are sinners and need a Savior to restore our relationship with a righteous God. While parts of New Age religion are true, the core of Christianity, what Jesus did on the cross for us and our need for a Savior to restore our relationship to God, is missing.

As Banquo told Macbeth in Shakespeare's famous play, "And oftentimes, to win us to our harm, the instruments of darkness tell us truths, win us with honest trifles, to betray us in the deepest consequence."

Weapons of Our Warfare

God never leaves us defenseless. He has given us effective weapons to fight the evil angels and has sent his mighty angels to guard us, fight for and with us, and bear us up when we are cast down.[103]

God sent his angels to comfort and strengthen Jesus after he was tempted in the wilderness (Matthew 4:11) and when he prayed in the garden the night before his crucifixion (Luke 22:43).

We can always pray for God to send angels to help us anytime we need strength to resist. Only when we get to heaven will we know how many times our lives were saved physically and spiritually by these holy angels who protected us. Praise God for them.

The Sword and the Shield

While the holy angels are mighty forces to assist us, we have a role in protecting ourselves and our loved ones from the enemy's designs and temptations. Jesus told his disciples, "See, I have given you authority to tread on serpents and scorpions, and over all the power of the enemy; and nothing will hurt you."[104]

Ephesians 6:11 tells us to put on the whole armor to God so that we can withstand the wiles of the devil. What is this armor that we are to put on? We are fighting a spiritual war, not a physical one. Different pieces of armor are required for this type of battle. First, we fasten the belt of truth around our waist. Truth trumps lies. God's Word is truth. When the enemy hurls lies at us (anything contrary to God's Word and will), we counter with truth. As noted above, this is exactly what Jesus did when Satan tempted him in the wilderness. As Satan was trying to get Jesus to worship him, promising Jesus all of the kingdoms of the world if he would, Jesus countered the temptation and the lies Satan told by quoting the Word of God (truth) to him. Jesus said, "Away with you, Satan. For it is written, 'Worship the Lord your God and serve only him.'"

We can do the same thing. When Satan tells me, "You don't have what it takes to do this job," I counter with, "My competence is from God."[105] Truth trumps the lie.

Another piece of armor we are to wear is the helmet of salvation. It is daily protection and deliverance from our sinful nature and Satan's schemes. Once we accept Jesus as our Lord and Savior, Satan has no hold on us.[106] Most of God's children do not know this, or at least they don't live like they do. When we keep our helmets securely fastened, Satan's fiery missiles cannot lodge and take up residence in our thoughts. With it, we can take every thought captive to obey Christ.

The sword of the Spirit is our offensive and defensive weapon. Since every Christian is in a spiritual battle with the satanic and evil forces of this world, we need to know how to handle the Word properly. Only then will it be an effective defense against evil, but it will also be an offensive weapon we use to "demolish strongholds" of error and falsehood.[107]

In Hebrews 4:12, the Word is described as living and active, sharper than a double-edged sword. Two edges make it easier to penetrate and cut in every way. Attacking with the Word drives back the forces of evil at play in any given situation. We must keep swinging.

I recently watched *The Robe*, a movie about a Roman centurion who crucified Christ. At one point in the movie, this centurion, who would later become a Christian and a martyr for the faith, fought another Roman who was seeking to break up a gathering of Christians listening to the Apostle Peter. The fight was fierce. It took the Roman defending the Christians many swipes with his sword against his adversary before finally gaining victory. Satan does not give up easily. We have to be determined and persistent.

What does this look like? Let's say I am afraid of a new situation I am facing. I have a choice. I can avoid the situation, go in with a defeated spirit, or confront it, recognizing where the fear comes from. I confront it by saying to Satan, "Get out. God has not given me a spirit of fear but of love, power, and a sound mind."[108] I will keep swinging my sword (telling the devil to get lost and quote the scripture) until he leaves. It works.

I've experienced the power of the sword many times. As I quote the Scripture, I envision its effect on the enemy by taking up the shield of faith, which "quenches the fiery darts of the enemy. In my mind, I see the arrows of fearful thoughts the enemy is hurling at me, deflected by my shield and falling to the ground. Swashbuckling with my sword and defending with my shield, I gain victory over the adversary. Fear leaves. Love, power, and a sound mind prevail.

Summary

The evil angels are formidable enemies. Because God loves us, He has given us weapons to fight their onslaught, and we are wise to learn about and use them. While our adversary is fierce and determined, we gain victory by using our spiritual weapons to fight for ourselves and those we love. We can ask God to send holy angels to help us anytime we feel attacked. As a precautionary measure, I pray Psalm 91 over myself, my family, and my friends every morning. That Psalm promises, "For he will command his angels concerning you to guard you in all your ways."

13

The Angels We Know and Love

"We are each of us angels with only one wing, and we can only fly by embracing one another."

Luciano De Crescenzo

We have seen how angels, which are spirits without bodies, can assume any form needed to aid us humans more times than we can imagine. They may appear as ordinary human beings, showing up exactly when we need them and with whatever it is we must have to save us from harm or help us out of a difficult situation. They may even appear as animals, light, music, or brute force.

God uses angels to minister to us, especially when no flesh and blood human is available to do the job. It is clear, however, that we humans are supposed to step up to the plate and minister to others whenever we can.

Jesus taught us to love our neighbor as ourselves. He told us stories about those who acted out this teaching. Perhaps the parable of the Good Samaritan (Luke 10:25–37) is the most famous and well-loved one. The victim, a man robbed and beaten, lay dying on the road. Religious leaders passed him by, but a man discounted by society as a half-breed, a Samaritan, stopped and ministered to him. The Samaritan bound up his wounds and took him to an inn where he could be cared for until he recovered. No heavenly angel was involved, just an ordinary man. God wants us likewise to render aid whenever we see a need.

Who are these flesh and blood angels? Let's look at some of them to inspire us to become better versions of earthly angels ourselves.

Firefighters, Police Officers, First Responders, Defenders of Our Country

Seven years ago, our house burned down. At 1:30 a.m., our phone rang. We did not answer it. It was our security company calling to tell us our smoke alarms were going off. The call woke us up, however, and I smelled something funny. I got up and followed the smell into our den. Walking into the den I saw fire breaking through the fireplace to the dining room wall. I yelled for my husband to call 911. We threw on our bathrobes, grabbed the dog, and got into one of the cars, backing it down to the street. My husband then backed the other car down as we waited for the firefighters to arrive, watching as the flames broke through the roof of our house and became more intense by the minute.

Within twenty minutes, three fire trucks and an ambulance appeared. The firemen jumped out and asked us if anyone or any pet was still in the house. We said no. At that point, these men charged into the flames with their hoses to extinguish the raging fire and keep it from taking down a neighbor's house with it. After about an hour, they had the fire out but warned us about hot spots that still existed.

We were numb from the temperature (16 degrees F) and the emotional experience. What stood out in our minds, however, was not how we felt but what these brave men had done for us. They had gone into a dangerous situation and put themselves at risk to take care of it, ensuring none of the neighbors' homes was destroyed. An ambulance came with the fire trucks.

When I mentioned to one of the firefighters that we did not request an ambulance, he said, "Ma'am, the ambulance is for us—a precautionary measure in case we need medical assistance on the job." I'm sure they often do.

A Few Good Men

Following the terrorist attacks of 9/11, Bill and Gloria Gaither put on a concert at Carnegie Hall, celebrating our country, our freedom, and those who gave their lives for us to be able to live as a free people. One of the songs, "A Few Good Men," underscored the courage and sacrifice the 343 firefighters who died in the Twin Towers made trying to help others. Here is a portion of the lyrics:

A FEW GOOD MEN

"What this dying world could use
is a willing man of God

Who dares to go against the grain
and works without applause;

A man who'll raise the shield of
faith, protecting what is pure;

Whose love is tough and gentle;
a man whose word is sure.

Chorus

Men full of compassion, who
laugh and love and cry–

Men who'll face Eternity and aren't afraid to die–

Men who'll fight for freedom and honor once again–

He just needs a few good men.

***

He calls the broken derelict whose
life has been renewed;

He calls the one who has the strength
to stand up for the truth.

Enlistment lines are open and He
wants you to come in–

He just needs a few good men.

Chorus

Men full of compassion, who
laugh and love and cry–

Men who'll face Eternity and aren't afraid to die–

Men who'll fight for freedom and honor once again–

He just needs a few good men."

As the singers sang the last verse, the Gaithers asked New York City Fire Department firefighters to come up on the stage in uniform. There was not a dry eye in the house as these responders walked up on the stage, the camera zooming in on the badges on their uniforms. People sprang to their feet, cheering wildly for these heroes who risked their lives every day to protect the people in their jurisdictions. Policemen and women, firefighters, first responders, and our men and women serving in the armed forces, all brave in dangerous conditions to protect others, are angels in human form.

Caring for the Marginalized

Dorothy Day was an American journalist, social activist, and devout Catholic who co-founded the Catholic Worker Movement in 1933 alongside Peter Maurin.

Her movement aimed to alleviate poverty and provide assistance to those in need, particularly during the Great Depression. Day and Maurin established "Houses of Hospitality," providing food, shelter, and clothing to the homeless and destitute. Day's commitment to serving the marginalized was deeply rooted in her faith and principles of social justice. She advocated for nonviolent activism, solidarity with the poor, and the importance of voluntary poverty. Throughout her life, she worked tirelessly to address issues such as homelessness, hunger, and social inequality.

Day's compassion and tireless efforts inspired countless individuals to join the Catholic Worker Movement and continue her legacy of compassion and service to those in need. Dorothy Day's life serves as a powerful example of selfless devotion to helping the marginalized access food, clothing, and shelter.

In twenty-first-century America, earthly angels continue to help the marginalized who need food, clothing, and shelter. Iowan Paul Erbes has been a team member and leader on twenty Habitat for Humanity builds from Fiji to El Salvadore. He says, "These projects are so fulfilling and energizing for me—plus they reflect my core beliefs. My signature Bible verse since I was young is Matthew 5:16, '…Let your light shine before others, so they can see your good works and glorify God.' For me, this means that I am driven to show God's love to others through my actions. This is how they can best see God."

Terri Gafford, from Wisconsin, agrees. She and her husband, Chuck, have built Habitat houses since 2007. "No matter where my husband and I are, our primary purpose is to work with families who are in need of decent housing. Their current circumstances prevent them from having this as a safe, decent, affordable foundational necessity."[109]

Other earthly angels serve the food insecure. Most Saturday mornings, Kent Coffland can be found somewhere in the Northern Illinois Food Bank warehouse sorting or packaging food for those in need. Kent began his volunteer career with some friends who came by two Saturday mornings a month to help out. Soon, he wanted to do more. Kent talked to the staff at the Food Bank and learned he could come every Saturday morning, which he started doing. Trading sleep to help others seemed like a small price to pay to be able to help those in need.

"I think volunteering makes me feel like I am helping make a difference in some small way. It makes me feel good to not only help those in need but also to sort of 'walk the talk' in terms of working at Feeding America...Every week, I see new and old volunteers and people who volunteer even more than I do regularly! Those folks are the unsung heroes of the food bank. I also stop and think about the impact volunteering can have. But then I stop and think that despite thousands of hours of volunteering done at the food bank, we are still not meeting the need to end hunger. In a nutshell, I think that is why I come back every week and will try to do so until one day in our future when there are no longer hungry people in need."[110]

Ministering to the Sick

Matthew's gospel foretells the judgment of the nations (Matthew 25:31–46) when all peoples will stand before Jesus and give an accounting of their lives. His sheep he will put at his right hand and the rest in his left hand. He will say to those at his right (sheep), "You are blessed and will inherit the kingdom prepared for you from the beginning of the world. When I was hungry, you gave me food; when I was thirsty, you gave me something to drink; when I was a stranger, you welcomed me; when I was naked, you gave me clothing; when I was sick, you took care of me; when I was in prison, you visited me."

The surprised sheep ask Jesus when it was that they saw him in such dire straits and ministered to him. Jesus replied, "Truly I tell you, just as you did it to one of the least of these who are members of my family, you did it to me."

Earthly angels follow Jesus' instructions. Some earthly angels go into caring for the sick professionally, which sometimes entails putting themselves at risk physically. During COVID-19, nurses, doctors, technicians, and others who work in hospitals braved a deadly virus to care for those who had the disease. Hoping their masks and protective gear would not fail, these earthy angels stared the lethal virus in the face to help those who had succumbed to it. Signs began to appear everywhere honoring these brave men and women, "Heroes work here." Yes, indeed.

Other earthly angels ministering to the sick visit patients in hospitals and nursing homes, write cards, volunteer to work in gift shops, pray with patients, take books and games around to long-term patients, deliver floral bouquets to the sick and shut-ins, and help the sick with various tasks they cannot do.

Still, others help raise money to provide health care for the marginalized and to enable research for cures of deadly diseases to continue. Angels write for websites to help those with diseases and start support groups to encourage those with certain illnesses. Others take food to the sick and their families, providing a needed service. Angels volunteer to babysit children while their parents are recovering. Dog lovers walk dogs and help the sick care for their animals. The list goes on and on. Creative human angels find many ways to obey their Lord.

Every little thing helps those who are struggling with a serious illness. My friend, Jane, had stage four cancer. We went to the same church and had worked together in a ministry for Hispanics where Jane was very helpful because of her ability to speak fluent Spanish. After rounds of chemotherapy and other therapies, she was finally sent home to die and put on home hospice. As I visited with her one day, her husband thanked me for a card I had sent her. "She lives for the mailman to come," he said. "Those get-well cards make her day." Human angels send cards and lift up prayers.

Visiting Those in Prison

Jesus included visiting those in prison in his list of compassionate acts his disciples should perform. Why is this? People in prison are criminals, the dregs of society. Who wants to visit them? Jesus. Jesus reached out to those scorned by society. He called a tax collector to be one of his disciples. He ministered to prostitutes, to half-breeds, to sinners, to women living in adultery, to uneducated, rough men. Jesus wants us to do the same.

Many of those criminals in prison are Christians. How did they get there? Terrible circumstances. Well-known Christian author and speaker Carol Kent shares her story in her powerful book *When I Lay My Isaac Down*. Carol's son, Jason, a graduate of the Naval Academy, married a woman with two little girls. She shared custody of the girls with the girls' father. When it became apparent their father was sexually abusing them, and no help was forthcoming from the courts, Jason confronted this man directly outside of a restaurant.

After heated words were exchanged, Jason pulled out a gun and shot him. He was convicted of murder and sentenced to life in prison.

Yes, Jason made a terrible and irreversible mistake. Yes, he has regretted it thousands of times, but no one can change what happened. Jason is a Christian. God has forgiven him. He assists the chaplain in his prison with chapel services. He has led other prisoners to Christ. God is using him right where he is.

Carol and her husband visit him regularly. While there they minister to the families of other prisoners. Carol's husband, Gene, takes trunks of T-shirts with them because they always meet someone wanting to visit a prisoner who is not dressed according to the prison dress code. They cannot get in to visit without more coverage. The T-shirt provides that.

Carol tells of being asked to speak at a prison, not where her son was, on Mother's Day. She was not getting good vibes from the chaplain who invited her. She felt he only extended the invitation because she was a mother, and he felt obligated. He told her she was the only woman ever invited to speak to the men there. Carol shared from her heart, telling the men about her son in another prison in their state. She sent out a mother's love to them and prayed she had made a difference.

After she spoke, two or three men approached her and said, "Mrs. Kent, we know Jason. He is the one who led us to Christ." One said, "He also helped me get my body back in shape through a great exercise program." (Prisoners are rotated from one prison to another for security reasons.) Carol broke down. She couldn't believe God was using her son in such marvelous ways.

While I have only visited prisoners twice, I have had prison pen pals for years. These men are so hungry for interaction with the outside world. Their families mostly ignore them. They need validation and loving concern. For Mother's Day this year, the only card I received outside my immediate family was from my prison pen pal. These men need someone to love. They need someone to share their hearts with. My pen pals have been Christians and they need encouragement with their ministries in the prisons where they are. I have encouraged one of my pen pals to try to get Bill Glass ministries, which does evangelical events for prisons, to come to his prison. He has a heart for some men there who have not yet found Jesus.

Carol Kent says that after her initial grief and deep sorrow at learning what her son did, she knew God wanted to bring good from it. She found ways to connect with other moms and dads whose children were in prison and bring hope to them. If we allow it, God will always bring beauty out of our ashes. Yes, human angels visit prisoners in person, through letters and emails, sending periodicals such as *Guideposts* magazines to them, or joining with groups such as church choirs to share the gift of music. As they do, they are blessed in many surprising ways.

Helping Travelers

Travelers are away from home in strange places. They don't have their normal support systems to help them if they have needs. Several states have created programs for those willing and able to help stranded motorists. Georgia's program is Highway Emergency Response Operators (HEROs). The yellow trucks, driven by the volunteers, can be seen on the side of the roads offering assistance at the site of accidents and helping any motorist with a need. They are our human angels in the yellow trucks.

My sister recently found herself stranded in the San Francisco airport when she missed her connecting flight and realized she could not get another flight out until the next day. She was returning home from Egypt, and her credit card was hacked and canceled. She had very little cash. The thought of spending the night in the San Francisco airport did not thrill her, but she saw no alternative until she mentioned her dilemma to the man behind her in the line to reschedule flights. This human angel did not hesitate for one second. He pulled out a wad of cash and said, "Here. Take this. You can get a hotel room."

My sister said it looked like several hundred dollars. She told him, "Oh, thank you, but I couldn't possibly take your money."

"Of course you can," he said, "I insist on it. I've got to go to the airport hotel myself to get a room, so let me go to the hotel with you and book your room."

My sister, in somewhat of a state of shock, took the short bus ride to the hotel with this Good Samaritan. He went to the hotel desk and booked two rooms, one for himself and one for my sister. He also made arrangements (and paid) for her to get a cab back to the airport the next day. My refreshed sister is now seeking a way to be a human angel herself to a traveler in need.

Summary

Human angels are all over the place, helping, encouraging, providing, packing, visiting, protecting, healing, and sharing gifts and talents with organizations that do good work. The funny thing is that as we practice being human angels to others, we ourselves receive the greater benefit. As the Apostle Paul, quoting Jesus, reminded the church, "It is more blessed to give than to receive."[111]

What if every one of us prayed to be a human angel to someone in our lives every day? Our spirit friends would enjoy some well-deserved time off!

Prayer

Angels are sent in divine service to those who are to inherit salvation.[112] If you are not sure you are one who will inherit salvation, please pray this simple prayer:

Dear Jesus,

I admit I am a sinner and in need of your gracious forgiveness. Please forgive my sins and come into my heart to be my Lord and Savior. Help me live the way you want me to, and bless me with angels to guide me to people and places where I can learn more about you.

Amen

Endnotes

1. Revelation 7:11–13.

2. Hebrews 1:14.

3. Mortimer J. Adler, *The Angels and Us* (New York, NY: Macmillan Publishing Co, 1982), 56.

4. Adler, *The Angels and Us*, 109.

5. L. W. Northrup, *Encounters with Angels* (Wheaton, IL: Tyndall House Publishers, Inc.), 16–19.

6. Adler, *The Angels and Us*, 132–136.

7. 2 Kings 6:8–23.

8. Revelation 12:2–4.

9. Nahum 2:3.

10. Psalm 91:11.

11. "Lt. Carey H. Cash (3)," Christian Evangelical City Church of Tallinn, February 20, 2024, https://www.citychurch.ee/lt-carey-h-cash-1/.

12. Peggy Joyce Ruth, *Psalm 91, God's Shield of Protection* (Brownwood, TX: Better Living Ministries, 2005), 147–148.

13. Exodus 33:1.

14. Numbers 22.

15. "The Hot Water Bottle," Missionary Sisters of St. Peter Claver, USA, accessed April 14, 2024, https://www.clavermissionarysisters.org/a-word-from-the-missions/stories-from-the-field/47-the-hot-water-bottle.

16. Personal testimony shared with the author on September 11, 2023, by Pastor Hiram Rosado Cintron and used with permission.

17. David Green, *Leadership Not by the Book*, (Ada, Michigan: Baker Books, 2022), 44–45.

18. Joan Webster Anderson, *An Angel to Watch Over Me* (New York, NY: Ballentine Books, 1994), 37–42.

19. Hope McDonald, *When Angels Appear* (Grand Rapids, MI: Zondervan Press, 1982), 87–88.

20. Northrup, *Encounters with Angels*, 107–108.

21. Howard Storm, *My Descent into Death* (New York, NY: Doubleday, 2005), 117–119.

22. Personal testimony shared with the author by Mark Newton in 2017, Atlanta, GA and used with permission.

23. Personal testimony shared with the author by her cousin (name changed for privacy) in July 2023 and used with permission.

24. Karen Goldman, *Angel Encounters* (New York, NY: Simon & Shuster, 1995), 159–161.

25. E. Lonnie Melashenko and Timothy E. Crosby, *In the Presence of Angels* (Boise, ID: Pacific Press Publishing Assn., 1995), 236–241.

26. Northrup, *Encounters with Angels*, 98–99.

27. Melashenko and Crosby, *In the Presence of Angels*, 47–51.

28. Hebrews 1:14.

29. Luke 15:19–31.

30. "God's angels are our personal escorts into Heaven," Opinion, Editorial Columns, The Brunswick News, August 25, 2016, https://thebrunswicknews.com/opinion/editorial_columns/gods-angels-are-our-personal-escorts-into-heaven/article_03fd12b8-3d50-5d5a-892a-6971ea2c6f49.html

31. Charles D. Bell, *Angelic Beings, Their Nature and Ministry* (London: The Religious Tract Society, 1895), 141–142.

32. McDonald, *When Angels Appear*, 109.

33. McDonald, *When Angels Appear*, 109.

34. Personal testimony shared with the author by Betty Powell, John Young, and Kathy Powell on December 17, 2023, and used with permission.

35. "Do Angels Take Us To Heaven When We Die?" Reasons for Hope* Jesus, accessed March 28, 2023, https://reasonsforhopejesus.com/do-angels-take-us-to-heaven-when-we-die/.

36. Judith MacNutt, *Encountering Angels* (Bloomington, MN: Chosen Books, 2016), 144–146.

37. Luke 16:31.

38. MacNutt, *Encountering Angels*, 137–139.

39. Psalm 23:4.

40. Genesis 24:40.

41. Personal testimony shared with the author by Eric Jackson in June 2023 and used with permission.

42. Melashenko and Crosby, *In the Presence of Angels*, 163.

43. Melashenko and Crosby, *In the Presence of Angels*, 164–165.

44. Goldman, *Angel Encounters*, 85–87.

45. MacNutt, *Encountering Angels*, 64–65.

46. Goldman, *Angel Encounters*, 103–106.

47. Ray Knighton, *Serving the Servants* (Darien, CA: Bookend Publishing, 2001), 81–83.

48. Joan Webster Anderson, *An Angel to Watch Over Me* (New York, NY: Ballentine Books, 1994), 30–36.

49. McDonald, *When Angels Appear*, 38.

50. McDonald, *When Angels Appear*, 65.

51. Judith MacNutt, *Angels are for Real* (Minneapolis, MN: Chosen Books, 2012), 127–129.

52. Anderson, *An Angel to Watch Over Me*, 100–105.

53. Personal testimony shared with the author by Dr. Robert Siegmann on April 7, 2023, in Atlanta, GA and used with permission.

54. Jude 1:9; Daniel 10:21; and Daniel 12:1.

55. Peter Kreeft, *Angels and Demons* (San Francisco, CA: Ignatius Press, 1995), 74–75.

56. Adler, *The Angels and Us*, 33.

57. Jude 1:9.

58. Isaiah 6:2–3.

59. "Angel Types in Judaism," Other Religions, Angels and Miracles, Learn Religions, accessed March 8, 2017, https://www.learnreligions.com/angel-types-in-judaism-123835.

60. Revelation 4:5.

61. Luke 1:19.

62. Tobias 12:15.

63. 1 Corinthians 13:12.

64. Harvey Humann, *The Many Faces of Angels* (Marina del Ray, CA: Devorss Publications, 1991), 15.

65. Humann, *The Many Faces of Angels*, 3–4.

66. Humann, *The Many Faces of Angels*, 5–6.

67. Adler, *The Angels and Us*, 73.

68. Revelation 5:11–12 (MSG).

69. Luke 2:9–14.

70. MacNutt, *Encountering Angels*, 115.

71. MacNutt, *Encountering Angels*, 116–117.

72. (see generally) Elfon Evans, *When He is Come: An Account of the 1858–60 Revival in Wales* (Bangor, Gwynedd, Wales: Evangelical Movement in Wales, 1959).

73. Isaiah 40:1, 49:13, and 60:13.

74. Personal testimony shared with the author by Virginia Sowell in November 2023 and used with permission.

75. John Conner, *The Angels of Cokeville and Other True Stories of Heavenly Intervention* (Murfreesboro, TN: Mamre Press, 1995), 149–151.

76. Richard Blackaby, *Encountering God Study Bible* (Nashville, TN: Thomas Nelson, Inc., 2006), 759.

77. Personal testimony shared with the author by Angel (last name withheld for privacy) on December 23, 2023 and used with permission.

78. Melashenko and Crosby, *In the Presence of Angels*, 37–38.

79. Melashenko and Crosby, *In the Presence of Angels*, 40–41.

80. Hope Price, *Angels* (New York, NY: Guideposts, 1993), 22–30.

81. Isaiah 37:15–20.

82. Isaiah 37:35.

83. "Were the Angels of Mons in World War I Real or Mass Hysteria?" Warfare History Network, August 2005 issue, https://warfarehistorynetwork.com/article/world-war-i-miracle-the-angels-of-mons/.

84. Melashenko and Crosby, *In the Presence of Angels*, 104.

85. Billy Graham, *Angels: God's Secret Agents* (Garden City, NY: Doubleday & Co., 1975) 165–166.

86. Zoe M. Hicks, *Oh, the Power: Prayers that Changed Nations and People* (Atlanta, GA: Encouragement Unlimited, Inc., 2019), 151–152.

87. "'Hand of God' prevents rocket from striking its target: Israeli Iron Dome operator says sudden gust of wind blew missile into sea when defence system failed," Daily Mail UK, updated August 6, 2014, https://www.dailymail.co.uk/news/article-2717659/Hand-God-prevents-rocket-striking-target-Israeli-Iron-Dome-operator-says-sudden-gust-wind-blew-missile-sea-defence-failed.html.

88. Melashenko and Crosby, *In the Presence of Angels*, 105–106.

89. Graham, *Angels*, 168–169.

90. MacNutt, *Encountering Angels*, 48–49.

91. McDonald, *When Angels Appear*, 85.

92. Revelation 12:7–9.

93. "Miracles seen from prayer," Tina Yeager interview, Linda Evans Shepherd's *Got To Pray*, YouTube, published August 15, 2023, https://www.youtube.com/watch?v=JknkRBykC7Y.

94. Tim Sheets, *Angel Armies on Assignment* (Shippensburg, PA: Destiny Image Publisher, 2021), 74–81.

95. Sheets, *Angel Armies*, 76–77.

96. 2 Timothy 1:7.

97. Matthew 14:22–36.

98. Mark 9:22–30.

99. 1 John 1:9.

100. Matthew 4:1–10.

101. Proverbs 18:21.

102. Deuteronomy 18:10–14.

103. Psalm 91:3–5 and 11–12.

104. Luke 10:19.

105. 2 Corinthians 3:5.

106. Romans 6:10.

107. 2 Corinthians 10:4–5.

108. 2 Timothy 1:7.

109. "Four volunteers build with four families across four continents," Our Work, Stories, Habitat for Humanity, accessed April 28, 2024, https://www.habitat.org/stories/four-volunteers-build-four-families-across-four-continents.

110. "My Passion for Volunteering," Hunger Blog, Feeding America, published January 15, 2015, https://www.feedingamerica.org/hunger-blog/my-passion-for-volunteering.

111. Acts 20:35.

112. Hebrews 1:14.

www.ingramcontent.com/pod-product-compliance
Lightning Source LLC
LaVergne TN
LVHW051836080426
835512LV00018B/2915